G000110037

JESUS: A NEW VISION

WHITLEY STRIEBER

Jesus: A New Vision
by Whitley Strieber

Jesus: a New Vision is a Walker & Collier book,

Copyright © 2020, Walker & Collier, Inc.

Walker & Collier Inc 20742 Stone Oak Parkway Suite 107

San Antonio, Texas, 78258

First Walker & Collier printing, first edition, 2020

Library of Congress Cataloging-in-Publication Data Strieber, Whitley

Jesus: A New Vision / by Whitley Strieber ISBN:

(Hardcover) 978-1-7342028-5-4

(Paperback) 978-1-7342028-6-1

(Electronic Book) 978-1-7342028-4-7

(Audio Book) 978-1-7342028-7-8

Cover design by Lisa Amowitz

Printed in the United States of America

First Edition

I wish to dedicate this book to two women, one who gave me life and faith, and the other whose wisdom sustained me through extraordinary difficulties, and who sustains me still.

Mary Strieber, 1915-1997
Anne Strieber, 1946-2015

I fled Him down the nights and down the days,
  I fled Him down the arches of the years
  I fled Him down the labyrinthine ways
  Of my own mind...

    Francis Thompson, "The Hound of Heaven"

TABLE OF CONTENTS

INTRODUCTION

We live in a wonderful and yet also a terrible time. As wonder piles on wonder, terror piles on terror just as fast. As our world gets more and more complex, we are left feeling ever more at sea. Almost without realizing it, the peoples of the world, especially in the West, have amassed amazing material wealth. While this journey into materialism has brought unprecedented comfort and safety, it has also drawn us away from the deeper and richer parts of our humanity, with the result that amid all this plenty, we are suffering a silent plague of loneliness. It is made worse by the dangers we face and the quiet dread with which most of us face death.

Our era may seem unique, but it is not. The Roman Empire was also struck by climate change, overpopulation, pandemics, mass migration and political turmoil. They did not understand the world well enough to survive, but we do. Still, their experience is incredibly instructive. Looking back into their troubles shines a bright light on our own, as we shall see.

They also experienced a terrible poverty of inner life, and their failure to feed the soul was a great part of their world's eventual collapse.

This book not only embraces the lessons of history, it takes a new look at inner life, one that is intended to be meaningful to us now, and to feed the emptiness inside us with a new kind of food.

Just when we most need to understand that our souls exist, new knowledge is making an ever stronger case that we are only physical beings. If we are blood and bone only, then the richness that we feel of life, the sense of purpose that drives us, is actually meaningless. Our lives, so complex and seemingly important as they are lived, are really nothing more than empty whispers in time.

In this book, I will explore a very different vision of what we are. I think that there is significant evidence that we are more than physical entities—that we are, in fact, moving through the stream of time in physical bodies in order to gather life experience into a timeless part of ourselves. It is our greater part, in fact, and its enrichment is our true purpose in life. But what about the quality of the experience we are offering to this hidden inner observer? When our physical bodies are used up, what do we want to take with us of the lives we have lived, and can we live in such a way that our harvest of days is a rich one?

Ironically, there is a teaching that reveals how to do this. In fact, there are many—all of the major religions offer sets of instructions. But this teaching is quite different. It demands much more of the disciple: rigorous inner search; living an outer life devoted to the good; questioning everything, even the pronouncements of the teacher. Especially those, in fact.

The teacher is Jesus, and the teaching I am describing has been lost.

Along with his real story, his actual message has been buried beneath a mountain of opinions that are promoted as facts. Hidden under all of that weight is not only a great and vibrantly accessible teaching that has the potential to profoundly enrich any human life right now, but also a human story that is far more extraordinary than has so far been told.

There are many beliefs about Jesus—that he was God as man, that he was a man with a special connection to God, that he was a spiritual master, that he was a revolutionary, even that he never existed at all. But none of them come close to the buried story that I seek to recover here.

What actually happened was far more amazing and important than anything that has so far been said about it by anybody, believers and nonbelievers alike. Always, there is an agenda, usually to prove either that he was God incarnate or that he was not.

I am trying to open a door to understanding his teaching in a new way that renews our inner lives and energizes our reason to exist. He said again and again that, if you followed his teaching you would "not know death." I think that I can show that this was not a metaphorical statement at all, but rather a completely new way of looking at life, death and afterlife—not only his own, but ours. Jesus was not just teaching a new way of living life. He was teaching a new way of transformation out of physical life, not just for him, but for all of us.

His teaching can enable us to experience the confidence and peace that comes with being craftsmen of our lives instead of simply wandering helplessly through the gaudy emptiness of the modern world.

He asks us to drop everything and follow him—which immediately challenges us to look at our lives and at his call, and ask ourselves what we really want out of life.

When that message became filtered through the dogma of Christianity's past, violence ensued. People forgot everything he taught about how to live on behalf of others and took up arms in defense of their beliefs. But, as will be seen, these people were desperately afraid. Their world was collapsing.

Millions of them were starving, millions more dying of plagues they thought were supernatural events. Strangers from outside their settled lands were pouring in and destroying their world.

It was their terror that turned them violent, not his message. They buried his most profound teachings in a grave of dogma and false beliefs. They literally buried the two gospels, those of Thomas and Mary, which contain the most useful insights into the path he was offering. I will discuss them for what they are and what they mean.

I have only one agenda here: to explore how we can use the teaching of Jesus and the example of his life to find our way out of the emptiness of our world and our lives. It concerns not only the emptiness of disbelief, though. It is also the about the emptiness of belief.

Jesus did not offer religious dogma. That was invented by others. So what did he offer?

There is another way of looking at his story and, at least for me, it has led to an explosive new vision not only of what he was, but of what a human being is.

He had stunning insight into what it means to be human. Indeed, his insight was so clear and so deep that he was arguably the greatest spiritual teacher who has ever lived. But to understand this teaching, we cannot use only the conventional story of his life. There is a deeper, more powerful and much stranger story hidden in the record—hidden in plain sight, actually. It is this story that I propose to tell here: why he intentionally went to his death on a cross and what actually happened after he was laid in his tomb, and what transpired over the centuries that followed, that transformed his vibrant teaching into yet another religion.

His passion was never intended to demonstrate that he was a god, separate from us and possessed of powers we can never hope to understand or attain. Rather, he was demonstrating through the enactment of his divinity—his defeat of death by returning from the tomb—how we can reach our own.

Because of the story of Jesus, a great and ancient civilization was destroyed and replaced. But how did it happen that an obscure carpenter from an obscure corner of a powerful empire played such a huge role in its collapse?

A whole civilization, with its beliefs, its gods, its temples and its vast knowledge was overturned and replaced by a new one. During this process, Jesus the teacher disappeared into Christ the god—a figure distant from us, demanding belief, and in possession of powers that we can never hope to understand, let alone attain. We are expected to follow him as a god, not learn from him as a teacher. This is wrong and we know it, which is why more and more of us are questioning the religious enterprise.

When we started to call Jesus a god we walled him off from ourselves. But this is the astonishing truth of his life: it was a demonstration of the fact that a human being had come into a state that is beyond life and death, and also an affirmation that any human being—any of us and all of us—can do exactly the same thing.

The canonical gospels are an attempt to identify him as a god, but I think that they actually do the opposite. The record as it is written shows not that he was a deity, but rather that he was a human being demonstrating human powers that have been buried within us by a huge dark wave of rejection and denial.

We are well into a time of upheaval that is startlingly similar to what befell Rome in the centuries after Jesus departed. This similarity is much greater than has so far been realized, and understanding how what happened to Rome relates to what is happening to us right now will also be central to my story. Understand, though, I am not saying that we are doomed to follow Rome. We have far greater resources at our command now. The Romans suffered climate change, mass migration, economic collapse and pandemics just as we do. But the Romans also had no idea how nature works or even what they themselves were. They attributed all fortune, good and bad, to their gods. They saw disease and disaster as supernatural punishments. During the series of pandemics that started around 150 A.D., millions upon millions of them died in agony, terror and ignorance. Fighting back, but with the wrong weapons, they replaced the gods they felt had failed them with a new one: Christ.

While Christianity has been a great good in the world, it also has a darker history. But why? What caused the movement to become intolerant? Does it have anything to do with the teachings of Jesus, or were there other forces at work?

Reading the accepted gospels with the eye of a detective reveals much that has been hidden more or less in plain sight. For example, it is clear that he intentionally goaded the Romans into killing him. I think that the reason he did this can be understood, as I will discuss.

He was also helped by a group of people who are almost invisible in the gospels, but not quite. They must have been incredibly learned. In fact, they must have known and understood the secret of death itself, and thus how to surmount it. They were not members of any known order, such as the Essenes. So who were they, and, for that matter, who was he, really?

Using a combination of a re-examination of his story and the application of scientific tools to, for example, study the Shroud of Turin, we can make exciting strides toward recovering the secrets that they must have known. Some of them are hidden in the Shroud, which, it would now appear, cannot have been a medieval forgery, as was incorrectly concluded back in 1988. As shall be seen, the evidence refuting that conclusion is strong. The implications of the resurrection event are amazing and exciting, and have something very new to say not only about Jesus, but about us.

Jesus is and has always been a great mystery. Our understanding of that mystery can now deepen. Much that has been hidden can become clear. We can find the meaning of Jesus in an entirely new way, and the time to do that is now.

1

RISING STAR

Three hundred thousand years ago, deep in a cave in what is now South Africa, a great mystery began. Something happened that marked the beginning of the human struggle with death, a struggle that has taken us on a long journey from magic to gods, to the strangeness and promise of Jesus, and more recently to a science of medicine that has at once prolonged life and, quite unexpectedly, opened a new door into the meaning of death.

All those eons ago, that rough place teemed with animals, including pre-human creatures like the powerful, ground-dwelling *Homo habilis*, and a smaller, more delicate and vulnerable creature which has been named *Homo naledi* (Man of the Star).

In the cave called Rising Star, there is a crevasse so narrow that only the slimmest person can slip through it. It leads down into a massive room that no four legged animal could reach. But a two-legged creature, small and lithe and possessed of hands, could manage the tortuous journey—just.

In September of 2013, two speleologists, Rick Hunter and Steven Tucker from South Africa's Speleological Exploration

Club, working under the direction of paleoanthropologist Lee Rogers Berger discovered—or rather, re-discovered—this unobtrusive crevasse that, through all the years that the cave had been known, had been overlooked—but not by everybody, not 300,000 years ago.

The only animal fossils in the chamber Hunter and Tucker found were the bones of a single owl. All of the other bones, hundreds of them, were from *Homo naledi*. It would seem that these ancient creatures, like us hominids, had been hiding their dead away in a place of safety.

Whether or not there was any ritual involved we will never know, but we can at once recognize the desire to cherish the bodies of our loved ones.

Hundreds of thousands of years later, the Egyptians were still reverencing their dead, but a good deal more elaborately: preserving their bodies as mummies, which were intended to remain as focal points in this world for the souls of the departed. To this day, many Christians, obedient to the promise that one day the dead will rise, seek to preserve their loved ones in sealed coffins. If the Shroud of Turin did indeed wrap the body of Jesus, then this piece of linen, which would have counted as a fine one in Roman times, would have been intended to confer upon his body exactly the same sort of respect that started so long ago in the Cave of the Rising Star.

Homo naledi had a brain only a third the size of ours. If you looked at one of them, you would see a small ape, rather more fragile than a chimp. It had very human hands, though, and what you would not see is that the brain, though small, was built much like our own.

Somewhere in that brain there appears to have existed the spark of self-knowledge that is the mark of the human, and with it the curse and the blessing that is our knowledge of death.

From that day to this we and death have been companions.

At the Shanidar cave system in Kurdistan are found more recent remains, from between 65,000 and 35,000 years ago, that suggest that Neanderthals, more advanced members of our line than *Homo naledi*, cared for their injured and their sick as well as their dead. There is a skeleton of a male who was badly injured but did not die of his wounds, and there are two cemeteries there that date from about 10,000 years ago and contain thirty-five individuals.

Also ten thousand years ago, *Homo sapiens* had advanced into symbolic construction. This was when the enigmatic Göbekli Tepe site in Turkey was created, with its beautifully carved dolmens. Also, the Sphinx at Giza, which will play such an enormous role in this story, may have been built at that time.

All of this, over this vast journey of ages, reflects the same thing: self-awareness and with it the emotions that cause us to miss our dead and mourn their passing.

With awareness of death came the sense of desperation that to this day shadows us all, which has given rise to the central human question: is there anything left of us after death, or is the richness of experience and mystery that is a human life doomed to simply disappear when we die?

When civilization began, we believed that only the highest born of us might experience an afterlife. Then Jesus appeared, bearing the stunning message that not only was there a realm of heaven in which all were equal, but that there was a path within us that could enable anybody who truly embraced it to bring the peace of that kingdom into their heart right now, before death.

The Jesus path is not a secret. It's laid out in the Beatitudes. But what has happened to the way we think about Jesus has caused it to be buried beneath an avalanche of confusion, misunderstanding and, finally and for most people who live in the formerly Christian Western world, indifference.

While an excess of Christian zeal destroyed the ancient

polytheistic religion that had grown up around the Mediterranean Basin, burned its books, pulled down its temples and in so doing tragically diminished human knowledge, it also began the development of an extremely powerful idea, which is that every human being is equal before God and therefore has equal value. As violent is it was, the Christian revolution gave us that.

For too many of us, the promise of the Jesus teaching has slipped away, encrusted in religious doctrine or dismissed because we find that doctrine impossible to accept. And yet the hope of some sort of deeper human validity is vividly alive in all of us, just as it was for *Homo naledi* or the builders of Göbekli Tepe or the apostles.

No more than we, the people of the past did not understand why death, or any disease or disaster, had to happen. They wanted to control their fate, but they had no means to do so. To fill the gap of ignorance, they imagined gods who had power over nature. They prayed to them and offered sacrifice.

The rise of science has caused belief in all gods, including Jesus, to fade in importance. Around the world, our deities are becoming more and more either sentimental figures, there to allow us the comfort of worship, or, too often, social totems used to justify political violence.

Presently, our world seems to be moving in many dangerous directions at the same time. It is hard to believe that we will not be facing more peril every day for years to come, and that Earth may eventually even become unlivable. As we shall see, that nearly happened to the Romans, and what did happen destroyed them.

Our earliest visions of how we understood our gods comes with the earliest written records that we can decipher, which appeared around 3500 B.C. There are earlier ones, such as the Danube script that is found in Central Europe and dates from the sixth millennium B.C., and the Easter Island script, but these have not been decoded.

The very earliest written records are basically business transactions. But then, around five hundred years later, texts such as the Pyramid Texts in the Pyramid of Unas in Egypt and, shortly after, the Epic of Gilgamesh appear. We go from recording simple contracts, lists of kings and possessions to creating works of great sophistication. Both are so highly developed that they suggest the existence of earlier texts that remain undiscovered.

The Pyramid Text contains a subtly drawn vision of the soul and its journey, and the way experience gathered in life feeds or poisons the soul. In the text, the spine is seen as a serpent of light that collects the experience of life and transmits it to the soul. When the body dies, the weight of the soul is measured against a feather.

The earliest known work of literature, appearing about a thousand years after the Pyramid Text, is the Epic of Gilgamesh. One of its sections is the first written account of the search for eternal life, which remains to this day a central human question, and is at the core of much religious doctrine. It is almost certainly why *homo naledi* protected their dead. They wanted to believe that there was a reason to do this, just as, hundreds of thousands of years later the Egyptians would mummify their dead and the Christian literature would promise that the dead will "rise incorruptible, and we will be changed." (I. Cor 15:52)

This desire for survival of the dead emerges out of self-awareness, and another remarkable ancient document commits to the written word with poetic intensity and devastating effect our discovery of the self. When we discovered ourselves, we also discovered death, and we began to plead for deliverance. We pleaded to gods we invented so that we could believe in our own prayers. But we were alone and we are still alone, and each one of us faces death alone.

Or do we?

The first record our discovery of self-awareness is the first three chapters of the Book of Genesis. It may have been written as early as the tenth century B.C., but most modern scholarship dates it to the sixth century. Its author is a matter of speculation, but its influence has been enormous. It can be said to be foundational to Jewish, Christian and Islamic visions of what human beings are, and how human beings are connected to, and relate to, God.

It records a creation story divided into an octave expressed as seven "days." On the fifth day it describes the creation of animals, and of man. God then gives man primacy over the whole creation and, at the beginning of Genesis 2, establishes us in a garden. That garden is the world as we knew it when we hunted and ate the fruits of the meadows. But the climate changed in the Middle East and became dryer. Solar output changed. Earth's orbit did, too. We explained it in the only way we could—as something that involved us. We decided that it was an act of God.

But why were we being punished? What had we done to deserve this catastrophe?

Ah, we had pleasure. That must be it. Our joy of life had angered a jealous God.

But why? Where did our pleasure come from?

Well, there was woman. And so comes a verse that has had one of the most negative effects of anything in sacred literature, or for that matter, all literature. It identifies woman as being created out of man, and explains her as the source of our fundamental sin of self-discovery. It thus justifies a fundamental social imbalance that, as Judaic tradition expanded into the Judeo-Christian and Islamic cultures that presently dominate so much of the world, has tragically stifled the influence of half our species on the advance of thought and culture.

Had women lived co-equally with men over these past millennia, it is not difficult to imagine that this might be a very different, more culturally rich and morally true world, not to mention a safer one.

The early Christian heresy that has become known as Gnosticism taught that the God of Genesis was a dark presence and saw Eve's taking of the fruit of the Tree of Knowledge as an act of heroism. This contention was a response to Genesis 3: 22, "And the Lord God said, 'The man has now become like one of us, knowing good and evil. He must not be allowed to reach out his hand and take also from the Tree of Life and eat, and live forever.'"

Now that a monotheistic interpretation of the Bible has become so ingrained in our thinking, it's easy to forget that the word "us" is used here. God is talking to somebody, but obviously it's not Adam, let alone Eve. Gnosticism asserted that enlightenment, or gnosis, was needed to see past the illusions generated by this dark god, and become one with the divine. As to who God was talking to, there has been much speculation, of course. The Book of Daniel makes reference to "watchers," or "messengers" who are described as angelic servants of God. The apocryphal Book of Enoch identifies them as watchers, some good and some evil.

Genesis also establishes man as having sinned against God —having "fallen"—a vision of the self which continues to haunt Western culture to its very depths.

Women, being the source of desire, were easy scapegoats for this supposed fall. If it hadn't been for Eve's tempting ways, Adam would never have been so foolish as to disobey the remarkably egotistical and neurotic god of the Old Testament. Because of Eve's supposed temptation, sexual pleasure became suspect, with tragic results that dog us still, in the form of the fear of women and sexuality that pervades Judeo-Christian and Islamic cultures. The belief that there is something wrong with sexuality and sexual pleasure has distorted billions of lives across a thousand generations, leading to the persistent condition of gender inequality in the West and the catastrophic subjugation of women in the Islamic world.

Genesis is also strikingly insightful, for, by describing the verses about Adam and Eve and their expulsion from Eden as he did, the Genesis author inadvertently created the first written account of the discovery of self-awareness. The time of its writing obviously does not mark the moment that this happened, but rather the first time an insight into it was recorded.

In Genesis 2:25, Adam and Eve "were both naked, and they felt no shame." In other words, they did not yet possess self-awareness. There is nothing to suggest that they were unintelligent, only innocent. Like animals, they lived without knowing what they were.

As Genesis 3 begins, we find a serpent lurking in a tree. This serpent, as we shall see throughout this book, is a very ancient symbol. In the Pyramid Text the spine is seen as a serpent of light.

The author of Genesis was promoting a new god, El, who would later merge into Yahweh, then Jehovah and now the omnipotent, formless God of the modern world. El was to be exclusive to the Hebrews, so the old ideas and the old powers had to be transformed into something evil in order to turn people away from them. Previous gods—in this case, those that had been brought out of Egypt—had to be reconceived as demons. Thus, what had been the light within us became the devil without. This process would happen again a few thousand years later, when the gods of the polytheists became the demons of the Christians.

In Genesis, the now-externalized source of knowledge ends up in a tree, which would, in the Egyptian religion, have been the body itself. The tree bears forbidden fruit—the knowledge of self. "When you eat of it, your eyes will be opened and you will be like God, knowing good and evil." In other words, when you know yourself, you will understand the consequences of your own actions and create your own moral universe. You will replace God with your own inner self. In Genesis, this is what brings on the wrath of the deity, who banishes humanity into an inhospitable region where they must plead for help from God in order to survive.

In the animal world, there is no good and evil. All animals are united in one thing: they behave only as they must, and in no other way. That behavior can be as simple as protozoans in a drop of water struggling to eat and be eaten to chimpanzees setting out on murder patrols in the jungle. It is behavior, but innocent—as indeed, in the days before we evolved a sense of self, our behavior was also without moral significance.

As our societies grew more complex, we began identifying certain behaviors as evil so that social order could be preserved. The person who followed a path supportive of the social order could expect a reward after death. Thus the forty-two laws of *ma'at* of the ancient Egyptians offered the promise of a path to heaven to anyone who upheld the social order. In the Papyrus of Ani, they are called negative confessions. The Ten Commandments, quite possibly compressed from them, are also, for the most part, negatives. And then come the Beatitudes, and suddenly there is a positive morality on offer. They are not about what we should not do in the world, but how the oppressed will be cared for by God. Because this necessarily suggests what we *should* do, that is to say, not be part of the oppression, it is a moral statement exponentially more subtle than the earlier ones. Far from being simple warnings, the Beatitudes require careful inner search to enact. You must observe yourself with love, compassion and humility to find out how they fit into your life. But doing so rewards the determined explorer with an entirely new vision of one's own life, not to say the whole human moral universe.

In Genesis, it is the realization that we are naked that triggers self-awareness. We might live naked as forest dwellers, but not in a larger social unit, not built as we are, unlike any other animal, hairless and bearing prominent, forward-facing genitals. We had to go clothed or overstress the fabric of society.

It was Eve who saw that the fruit of the forbidden tree was "good for gaining wisdom." Eve is a reversal of the Egyptian goddess Isis, insofar as she has the exact opposite of the goddess's attributes. Isis is immortal while Eve is mortal. Isis possesses wisdom while Eve tries to steal it. It has to be this way, of course, as Adam cannot be the one to blame for stealing knowledge from God.

So, as Genesis 3 comes to its conclusion, we are made aware in no uncertain terms of what self-knowledge has brought us, "for dust you are, and to dust you will return." (Gen. 3:19) The timeless world of our innocence is at an end.

The earliest written record clearly concerning human self-awareness that we have thus contains a group of flaws that have worked ever since to distort that very awareness. But why is it like that? Why is our discovery of ourselves distorted like this? After all, the story could have been a joyous one—a god expressing delight that the pinnacle of his creation can know him. Instead, the god of Genesis is so angry at our evolutionary success that he drives us into a desert where we end up scratching for a living and fighting among ourselves like rats in a maze.

Thus begins the relationship with deity that has been with us ever since. Supplied with everything, we don't need gods. Supplied with nothing and not understanding why, we are going to invent them.

There were numerous climatic upheavals beginning 12,000 years ago when the last ice age ended. It's possible that the worldwide legends of great floods reflect the sudden melting of the glaciers, and that a story of people living in a garden of plenty that became a desert memorializes one or more of the abrupt climate upheavals that took place between 12,000 B.C. and 5,000 B.C.

As the authors of Genesis had no understanding of nature, they assumed that a power greater than any they could control must be responsible for natural disasters. There could be only one such power: God. From time immemorial, nature's power has been personalized as the action of gods. All religion, in one way or another, is based on controlling gods with sacrifice and prayer—all religion, that is, until the time of Jesus, who spoke not just in terms of satisfying God, but also entering into a companionship.

Sacrificing to gods has nothing to do with controlling nature and therefore must often fail. When it does, a sense of guilt is generated. When you sacrifice a valuable animal and the rain doesn't stop, you naturally feel that you have not satisfied your god. You up the ante, perhaps sacrificing a child. When things get worse and worse no matter what you do, you are eventually going to conclude that there is something fundamentally wrong with you, and before you know it, your society has institutionalized an idea like original sin. In our case, this unfortunate mistake has deprived generation after generation of the chance to fully embrace the joy of being alive and being human.

As the ice age ended, climate upheavals caused mass extinctions and diebacks. In areas such as the Middle East, humans had to abandon hunting and gathering and start growing food for themselves. That this was hard for us is revealed by the difference between the bones of hunter-gatherers and those of early farmers. The farmers are smaller and show signs of diseases like rickets and arthritis that are not seen in the hunter-gatherer fossils.

The human journey has come to another turning point that is very similar to the one that we experienced when the ice age ended. Just as the people of those distant times had to either starve or figure out how to farm, we are going to have to figure out how to cope with the extinction event that is unfolding now, or suffer the consequences. But what can this have to do with a teacher from a distant time, whose short career ended in an ignominious death on a cross?

What he left behind is an idea of who we are that we have never really understood or perhaps been able to face. Time has run out. If we are to survive, we must face his real message, and we must understand. Its value is attested by the strangest and most hopeful thing about his life, the one thing that suggests that there may actually be something on offer to mankind from a higher entity that, for want of a better word, we might as well call God.

It is the extraordinary fact that he is remembered at all.

2

JESUS IN HIS WORLD

Jesus was born in a hard place in a terrible time. A few years before his birth, in the year 37 B.C., a catastrophe had befallen the Jews of Palestine. In that year Herod the Great, an Arab, was set up as their king by the Romans and they lost the last vestige of their independence. The Romans, with Herod as their surrogate, imposed a brutal and costly regime on them that would lead, in 66 A.D., to the revolt that would destroy Jerusalem and its great temple, and disperse the Jewish nation for what would turn out to be two millennia of wandering in a hostile world.

In the two hundred years prior to Jesus's birth, which appears to have taken place around 5 B.C., the entire Mediterranean world had been upended in what remains the greatest act of pillage in human history. Rome was a thief, and what it was stealing was entire nations, and it was stealing them from themselves. Originally just one of a number of Italian city-states, it gradually gained control of the entire boot of Italy, then spread its dominion across the Mediterranean basin, bringing with it brutal rule and a confiscatory system of taxation designed to impoverish local people and force them into debt, causing them to lose their lands to the Roman holders of their notes.

Most conquered nations experienced Rome only as an economic pirate. The Roman historian Tacitus quotes a speech made by the rebel Calgacus, who was killed in a battle with the army of Gnaeus Agricola in northern Scotland in 83 or 84 A.D. Calgacus called the Romans "robbers of the world" and said of them, "To plunder, butcher and steal—these things they mistake as empire: they create a desolation and call it peace."

To the Jews, Roman control was not only an economic disaster, but also a religious nightmare. Rome was a polytheist power that demanded a show of loyalty to its own gods, not only by conquered states, but also by individuals, who were expected to give public sacrifice to the deified Roman emperor.

Many, but not all, Jews believed that their god demanded exclusive worship. As he was a disincarnate entity, they felt his presence within themselves, and so experienced a deeper crisis of faith than did other Mediterranean peoples when made to worship against his laws.

Alone among the temples in the Mediterranean world, the inner sanctum of the temple in Jerusalem contained no statue. In the Parthenon in Athens, there sat a huge, vividly painted statue of the goddess Athene, which was, as was true throughout the region, worshiped as if it *was* the goddess. On the Capitoline Hill in Rome, the Temple of Jupiter contained an immense statue of Rome's most powerful deity, Jupiter, like all the others in all the other temples across the whole region, also believed to embody the god.

When a worshiper completed his sacrifice and left one of these temples, he also left the god behind.

Perhaps the Jewish god's disincarnate nature arose out of the fact that the Jews had been, in earlier times *haibru,* wanderers, and so could not house him in any fixed place. Even when they did find a homeland among the Canaanites, their god did not acquire a physical shape.

Hoping to live in peace, many Jews—in Jerusalem itself, probably most—accepted Roman rule and enacted the necessary sacrifices. Upper class co-operation with the Romans would eventually lead Jesus to do violence in the temple precinct itself, which was what brought on his execution.

Rebellion was always a temptation in the Roman Empire. This was because the Romans generally garrisoned their possessions with the smallest possible number of troops, instead giving the local upper class a share of the taxes levied, thus making them at once rich and dependent on Rome for survival. It would then rely on them to maintain order. Roman soldiers were not often seen except when a few of them might accompany an official, protecting him as he moved around. To an individual living far from a strong point, Roman power would have seemed rather theoretical—that is, until the tax collector showed up and claimed half to three-fourths of everything he produced. He would be stripped of his possessions and left to starve unless he went into debt. Soon, he would be selling his children and even his wife in the slave markets. Even if his family survived intact, as the debt overwhelmed him, he would wind up living as an indentured servant on land that, in many cases among the Jews, would have been in the care of his family from time immemorial. The Jews did not believe that they owned the land they worked. Only God owned the land. So when the Romans claimed it, to the Jews they were taking it from God, as horrible a blasphemy as they could imagine.

Even the relief from debt brought by the loss of a farmer's land to a Roman landowner would not improve his situation for long, for his Roman master would begin demanding that cash crops like olives and grapes and wheat be planted, leaving him only the bare minimum acreage on which to raise food for himself and whatever family he still had.

A flood or a drought or a wildfire during harvest season would leave him and his family to starve, and in a region with a marginal climate, disruptions were frequent. The farmer, facing death, had only one choice left, which was to sell members of his family. This was legal under Roman law, and even four hundred years after the life of Jesus was still a common practice. In 368, Basil, the Bishop of Caesarea on the Judean coast, described such a situation. The desperate farmer "turns his eyes at last to his children, to take them to the market and find a way to put off death...He goes, and with ten thousand tears, sells his most beloved son."

It is easy to forget the reason that Basil would even think to write those words. He could do so because he was following the new moral order that was based on the teaching of Jesus that every human being had value and mattered to God, and for a man to be compelled to sell his child was not only horrible, it was a moral evil.

Because of the pillage and what the Jews regarded as the institutionalized blasphemy of Roman rule, during the childhood of Jesus Galilee and parts of Judea were a tinderbox of revolutionary fervor. As the people were entirely helpless, they began to respond to leaders who claimed that, by re-enacting Moses' march into Canaan, they could evoke God's power just has he had done, and drive out the Romans without an army. In around 90 A.D., the Jewish historian Josephus wrote in *Antiquities of the Jews* about a "charlatan" called Theudas who attempted to persuade people to take their belongings and follow him to the Jordan River, cross it and re-create Moses' march into Canaan. The Roman procurator Cuspius Fadus sent out a company of cavalry to stop them. The soldiers killed many of them and, as Josephus reports, returned to Jerusalem with the head of Theudas.

A mysterious figure called "the Egyptian" tried something similar in the year Jesus was born. His followers were also massacred. There were so many other "messiahs" that an exasperated Pontius Pilate, a brutal man who neither understood the sensitivities of the Jews nor wanted to, finally crucified one of them, known as "the Samaritan," simply for hinting at sedition.

At the time of Jesus's birth, Sepphoris, the city closest to Nazareth, was known as "the Jewel of Galilee." Sepphoris means "bird," and the city may have gotten that name because it is perched on a hill. It is a lovely, breezy spot to this day, and the elegant little Roman amphitheater there is a haunting reminder of a once bustling community.

When Herod the Great died in 4 B.C., he left behind an unhappy population, including a large number of workmen in Jerusalem who were left unemployed when his extensive building program was halted. Many of these were former farmers who had descended into the laborer class because they had lost their farms to debt. They were not allowed to stay in the city, but instead were driven out to the countryside where they found themselves penniless and hungry and unable to feed their families.

The result of this was a general upsurge in banditry, robbery and burglary throughout the region. In Galilee, another revolutionary appeared, this one called Judas. He gathered a large force around him and began to pillage the countryside. Himself the son of a failed messiah called Hezekia, he was also a religious leader and created a new movement called the "Fourth Philosophy." The Fourth Philosophy, unlike the other three, which were the Pharisees, Saducees and Essenes, was fanatically determined to rid Israel of the Romans. In a region teeming with miserable and desperate people, Judas was soon in command of a small army. They laid siege to Sepphoris, broke in and looted its armory. Joined by many from the city, they ranged through Galilee killing and stealing the belongings of anybody suspected of complicity with Rome.

Over a ten year period, the movement grew in size until, in 6 A.D., when the Quirinius, the governor of Syria, declared a census in anticipation of setting up a system of taxation, Judas responded by declaring that paying taxes to Rome amounted to honoring their gods, which no Jew must do.

As would happen again when Jesus attempted to disrupt the temple economy that fed money into the Roman purse, Rome reacted by capturing and killing Judas, then marching on Sepphoris. They burned the city, slaughtered the men, and auctioned off the women and children as slaves. Josephus reports that two thousand men were crucified in the hills around the sacked city.

If Jesus was indeed born in Nazareth, as most modern scholars believe, he would have grown up hearing stories of a Roman desolation. The little hamlet was a couple of hours walk from Sepphoris.

If the scholars are correct, then it must also be correct that Joseph was a carpenter and that Jesus, along with his brothers, worked in their father's shop. In the social hierarchy of the time, a landless craftsman was lower than a farmer, which would mean that Joseph and his family were at the bottom of the social ladder in Nazareth, below the farmers and above only the slaves—if there were any in this community of perhaps ten or twelve families.

In the gospels, the word used to describe Joseph's occupation is *tekton*, a Greek word that can mean anything from carpenter to engineer or even teacher.

Archaeologists have found very little that can be traced to the Nazareth of the early years of the first century. There are no foundations, no carvings, and no sign of any large houses. Some caves in the area were inhabited, and fronted by structures where animals were kept and food was prepared. The free standing houses were constructed of fieldstones, probably faced with plaster. The floors were of beaten earth. As no roof tiles have been found, the roofs would have been wooden, probably thatched. There was no synagogue, so when Jesus taught there, if he did, it would have been in one of the houses, or more probably, in the open air of the town center. Ken Dark of Reading University has been studying a Nazareth house for 14 years and concludes that it was typical of the period, a simple, well-crafted structure.

The people of Nazareth had little. We know this because the only coins found there dating from the period are bronze, the least valuable. The few personal decorative items that have been recovered are beads and trinkets. Pottery was locally made. There were vines grown on trellises and olive groves on the rocky hillsides. Grinding stones still remaining show that olives were crushed for oil. Barring drought, wheat, millet and barley were grown in fields below the town. Vegetables and legumes were planted on terraces, which were irrigated by the little creek that ran through the center of the community. The headwater of this creek is now known as Mary's Well, and still flows. There are now two churches near the well, but there is no evidence from the time of Jesus that there were any public buildings there. The whole town was contained in the space that now lies between the churches and the well, which is a distance less than half a mile.

The tombs in the area confirm that the town was Jewish, as body shafts, or *kokhim*, have been carved into the hills, more modest examples of the quite grand one near Jerusalem where Jesus would be interred after his crucifixion.

It is unlikely that anybody in Nazareth would have been literate. The literacy rate in the early Roman Empire was around 5 percent except in large cities, but even there it is doubtful that it reached more than 30 percent. There would have been no reason for somebody who had reading and writing skills, valuable in a city but useless in a rural community, to reside in Nazareth.

It is hard to understand the depth of poverty and human vulnerability that characterized the world in ancient times. Even in the cities, half of all children were dead before they were five, and most of those who survived were worn out by their late thirties. So Jesus, when he began teaching at the age of thirty-two, was already in the last decade of an average life.

Perhaps his awareness of his advancing age was one of the things that motivated him to begin his ministry.

On the surface, it started with a journey to see John the Baptist, who was then teaching on the banks of the Jordan River, baptizing converts in its waters. Jesus went to hear him and be baptized, and returned home on fire with zeal.

Mark 6:3 reports that many of his neighbors were more than a little surprised at the change in him. "'Is not this the carpenter, the son of Mary, the brother of James, and Joses, and of Juda, and Simon, and are not his sisters here with us?' And they were offended at him."

There is a surprise in that brief passage in this earliest of the gospels. It is that phrase "the son of Mary." Naming him the child of the mother rather than the father meant that he was thought to be born out of wedlock. This lends credence, if not credibility, to the story of the virgin birth, but also demands consideration of the other, more prosaic stories of Jesus's actual patrimony, and perhaps explains the strange anger and bizarre violence that seems to have characterized his childhood.

Mark is the only gospel to omit Joseph as the father. By the time Luke and Matthew come along, the importance of this omission has been realized, and these authors are careful to include him. In the description of the same incident in Matthew 13, the neighbors ask "Isn't this the carpenter's son, isn't his mother's name Mary..." In Luke, the last of the synoptic gospels, the author is careful to change the text from "Mary's son" to "Joseph's son" (Luke 4: 16-20).

This was important at the time the later gospels were being

written, because the Jesus-as-messiah story was developing, and, virgin birth or not, if he had not been accepted as being of Joseph's lineage, then he was not descended from the House of David, and thus could not be the prophesied messiah. Both Micah and Zechariah had said that it would be a descendant of David who would restore Israel (Mic. 5:1-5 and Zech. 9:1-10).

It went deeper than that, though. If he was to build a kingdom that was in covenant with God, the messiah had to have the same connection to the deity that Moses did. For this to be believed, the birth story of the messiah would need to follow, at least in broad outline, the birth story of Moses, and this is exactly what happens in the canonical gospels.

In Exodus 1-2, the pharaoh decrees that all newborn Jewish males must be killed because the population was growing too fast. Moses is saved by his own sister, who raises him as an Egyptian. By the first century A.D., this basic story had been expanded. In *Antiquities of the Jews*, Josephus relates a story that was circulating in his time, and thus may well have been known to Matthew. In this story, a scribe who understood how to predict the future tells the pharaoh that a child will be born among the Hebrews who will overshadow the Egyptian royal line. This is why the pharaoh orders the massacre of the children recorded in Exodus. Moses' father, Amram, described by Josephus as "a Hebrew of noble birth," prays for help in saving his soon-to-be-born child from Pharaoh's knife. He is told that the baby will be visited by a miracle. Pseudo-Philo, the unknown author of *Biblical Antiquities,* written somewhere between the middle of the first and second centuries, has Moses's sister Miriam dreaming that the child yet to be born will lead the Hebrews and work miracles.

In reading the gospels, it must be remembered that they are not history. In the minds of the authors, it was reasonable to invent stories to fulfill prophecy. The reason for this is that they did not have firsthand knowledge of the actual life of Jesus, and therefore assumed that, since he was the messiah, events that supported this belief must have happened even though they had no factual evidence.

There are hints in the non-Christian literature that a more ordinary sort of a life was known at the time. The story of Jesus' birth and early life recorded by the anti-Christian author Celsus in his book *On the True Doctrine,* written around 177 A.D., differs quite dramatically from the gospel version.

We know Celsus's book only from a later refutation, *Contra Celsum,* written by the Christian author Origen Adamantus. All copies of the original have disappeared, presumably burnt during the catastrophe that befell the old polytheistic culture when Christianity replaced it as the official Roman religion in the fourth century. By examining Origen's refutations, the contents of Celsus's original story can be deduced.

Origen was himself declared a heretic and his books also burned, but fortunately some copies survived. Without them, Celsus would have disappeared from history. Once the church became an official institution, it wanted stories that could inspire faith by being seen as factually true. So the canonical gospels, despite their many differences and contradictions, became a sort of false biography of Jesus.

Celsus, who probably understood perfectly well the seductive nature of a story that started with a miraculous birth and ended with a resurrection from the dead, set out to strip away any suggestion of miracle from the birth narrative. In his book, he counters the magical story with a more prosaic one— ironically, one that is probably more likely to be true than impregnation by an angel. As this story goes, Mary was "turned out" by Joseph when he heard of her pregnancy, because the child she bore was fathered by a Roman soldier called Pantera.

According to the Protoevangelium of James, a second century apocryphal text, and much Christian tradition, Mary was presented in the temple during her twelfth year by her parents, Joachim and Anne. Although it is not mentioned in any of the Christian texts, sacred prostitution was common in the ancient world, but it's not clear that it was being practiced in the Temple of Solomon at the time of Mary's tenure there. If it was, though, then Celsus's claim may have some substance.

Origen says that the claim has its origin in rabbinic literature, and the Christian author Tertullian around the year 200 A.D. sums up the Jewish account, which has Jesus as "the son of a prostitute" who, after he had been placed in his tomb was either taken by his followers or gotten rid of by the gardener "lest his lettuces be damaged by the crowds of sightseers."

There was a soldier, Tiberius Julius Abdes Pantera, whose tombstone has been found in Germany. He could have been stationed in Palestine during the early years of the Christian era. But Panther was a not uncommon name taken by soldiers, and there remains no way to determine what really happened. I don't think an unusual birth story should be dismissed out of hand, either. As we shall see, it is as much a mistake to "secularize" Jesus by dismissing the miracles and the resurrection as it is to take the gospels literally.

Mary and Joseph are mentioned many times in the canonical gospels as Jesus's parents, without reference to a virgin birth, and the Protoevangelium states that Mary was married to "a rich carpenter" named Joseph after she completed her term as a temple virgin. Saint Augustine explains the apparent contradiction between the virgin birth and the fatherhood of Joseph by saying that, as he was Mary's husband, he would have also have been regarded as Jesus's father even though he was not his of "his seed," as Augustine puts it.

Matthew, writing around fifty years after the crucifixion, knew that he could not allow Mark's earlier revelation that Jesus was an illegitimate child to stand, not if he was to convince the Jews that he was indeed the messiah. To make matters worse, all the instances of divinely inspired births in

the Old Testament involve unexpected pregnancies in women
who have already carried children, not virgins.

So how to get around this? Fortunately for him, there were
stories of virgin births in other religious traditions in the
Mediterranean world. The recently deified emperor Augustus
was said to have been conceived by his mother Atia after she
fell asleep in a temple of Apollo and was impregnated by a
huge serpent—the god in that most provocative of forms, so
familiar from the Bible, the Pyramid Text, and so many others.

Suetonius, the author of *The Lives of the Twelve Caesars,* says
that the story of Augustus's divine father came from Egypt and
started around 30 B.C., meaning that it would have been
universally known in the empire by the time the gospel authors
were writing.

Matthew erred when he quoted Isa 7:14, "Therefore the
Lord will give you a sign: the virgin will conceive and give birth
to a son, and she will call him Emmanuel." He was a Greek
speaker and therefore was quoting the Greek text. The Hebrew
text uses the word *almah,* which means "young woman," not
necessarily a virgin. But in the Septuagint, the Greek translation of the Hebrew Bible which Matthew would have known,
the word is trans-lated as *parthenos,* virgin. Thus another
wrinkle is added here: Matthew did not need to identify Mary
as a virgin in order to relate Jesus to prophecy, but he did not
know this.

It cannot be forgotten that in the gospels we are looking at
both political statements and spiritual teachings, which obviously have very different purposes. But they have been mixed
over time so completely that Christians in the present era
must simply swallow the idea that the Prince of Peace who
said, "Peace I leave you; my peace I give to you," also said, "do
not suppose that I have come to bring peace to the earth. I
did not come to bring peace, but a sword."

As the messiah was prophesied to be both a physical ruler

and a spiritual master, Jesus had to be both a physical king willing to lead his people to war and a spiritual one able to lead them to heaven. So the story that we have relies on a foundation in myth, prophecy and tradition intended to at once establish the earthly authority of this Jewish competitor to the Roman state, and to reveal him as the messenger of a new spiritual destiny that overrides the Roman state divinity. As we shall see, it is further complicated by the addition of stories from the other religions of the period, in particular those of the solar deities.

While the story of Herod's slaughter of the innocents is meant to show the life of Jesus paralleling that of Moses, it is not impossible that Herod might actually have hunted for the infant Jesus with the intent of killing him. Although, given the restlessness of the Jews under Roman domination and how much Herod was despised, it is unlikely that he would have risked carrying out a campaign as unpopular as the mass murder of firstborn boys would have been. The Romans chose their local leaders for their ability to keep the peace and not cost the empire more to keep order in a province they ruled than it was returning in taxes. If Herod had done something that caused an uprising, such as killing thousands of children, his rule would have come into question in Rome.

If Jesus was not born the child of humble Nazarenes at all, but of a noble family that actually did claim lineage back to David, Herod might well have wanted to kill him. The reason would have been that the Romans would have seen such a child as a potentially more popular ruler, and gotten rid of Herod in favor of a Jesus regency.

Anyone hearing the Jesus story during and immediately after his lifetime would have found it astonishing that an illiterate peasant from a simple hamlet like Nazareth could have acquired the education necessary to make pronouncements such as he did, that emerged so very subtly out of Torah, and went beyond Torah. What could be the explanation except that he was a divine presence disguised as an illiterate *tekton*— unless, of course, the story of the peasant child from Nazareth is meant to disguise a genuine royal child who was the heir to an anti-Roman Jewish royal line, and thus had to be hidden from both Herod and the Romans.

The magi story in Matthew may be an indication of this. About fifty years prior to the birth of Jesus, Parthia, now Iran, had taken advantage of the turmoil in the Roman Empire that followed the assassination of Julius Caesar to briefly capture Judea. It was recaptured by Rome just a few years later, and there seems an outside possibility that the Matthew story could be drawn from the memory of a Parthian embassy sent to honor the newborn Jewish heir, in hope that he would, in the future, favor good relations with Rome's enemy.

Many scholars discount the idea that Jesus was born in Bethlehem, although the story appears both in Matthew and in Luke. The fact that there is no birth story in Mark suggests to them that it was a later invention, but if Jesus was believed by the Romans to have been an anti-Roman pretender, when Mark was written it may have been safer to simply leave out any birth story that suggested that he might be a royal person. This would have been done to protect his family. Years after his crucifixion, in fact, some of them were interrogated as to a possible royal origin, but this came to nothing.

Luke says that Joseph took Mary with him to Bethlehem in response to a requirement to register as part of an empire-wide census decreed by Augustus. But the only census recorded from the period is that of Quirinius in 6 A.D. However, even though Judas the Galilean used it to inspire his uprising, the census did not include Galilee where Nazareth was located, but covered only Judea, Samaria and Edom (Greek Idumea). This meant that Joseph, a Galilean, would not have incurred any obligation to be recorded in it.

No known census would have compelled Joseph to go anywhere.

There was also the crisis in Galilee and the fact that Judas and his followers might well pillage a little community like Nazareth, which would have been full of men who had worked on Herod's projects in Sepphoris. Women, especially those of child-bearing age who did not have husbands, were likely to be raped or kidnapped into forced marriages.

Luke identifies Mary not as Joseph's wife but as his betrothed. Under Jewish law, this meant that she had the rights and obligations of a wife, but also that her future husband did not yet have the right to make her pregnant. The law was like this because child marriages were common in that time and there had to be a way of preventing a pregnancy from happening before a girl's body was mature enough to safely bring a baby to term.

Even though she was not yet of age to marry, as a betrothed, Mary was bound by the marriage law, which meant that, if she became pregnant by another man, she was an adulteress and subject to humiliation and potentially criminal penalties. Add to this the fact that Sepphoris was likely to be attacked by the Romans, and there are quite a few reasons that Joseph might have decided to become a refugee. With Nazareth only a few hours' walk from Sepphoris and his fiancée subject to ostracism or worse if her pregnancy was discovered by his neighbors in their small town, it would not be surprising that he left the area and took her with him.

It has been speculated that Mary was Joseph's second wife, but if they indeed travelled as refugees to Bethlehem, it seems more likely that she was his first, and Jesus the first son. This is because nowhere in any of the gospels are his sisters and brothers described as being with the couple in Bethlehem. Still later, when the family is claimed to have gone to Egypt, no other children are mentioned. Matthew, Luke and Mark all mention a family, but not in the context of Jesus's birth or the possible journey to Egypt. The first acknowledgement of their existence comes in Matthew 13:55 when Jesus returns from his time with John the Baptist, and James, Joseph, Simon and Judas are identified as being his brothers. By then, Jesus would have been in his late twenties, or perhaps as old as thirty. In Luke 2:7 as well, Jesus is called the firstborn of Mary. The only direct mention of Joseph having an earlier wife appears in Celsus.

Celsus's condemnation of Jesus for his low birth refutes Luke's claim that he was born in Bethlehem in fulfillment of prophecy. "Is it not true, sir, that you fabricated the story of your birth from a virgin to quiet rumors about the true and unsavory circumstances of your origin? Is it not the case that, far from being born in royal David's city of Bethlehem, you were born in a poor country town, and of a woman who earned her living by spinning? Is it not the case that when her deceit was discovered, that she was pregnant by a Roman soldier called Pantera and not by her husband the carpenter, he drove her away... Indeed, is it not so that in her disgrace, wandering from place to place, she gave birth to a male child in silence and humiliation?"

So either he was born of a disgraced woman whose husband was an illiterate carpenter but nonetheless somehow acquired incredible learning, or he was of higher birth and the story of the humble carpenter was put about during his lifetime to protect him and his family, and picked up as true by the gospel authors, who knew only the public narrative and were unaware of the secret it concealed.

The identification with Bethlehem (The House of Bread) also relates Jesus to another resurrected deity, Adonis. Much later, in the fifth century, Saint Jerome writes in Letter 58, "Bethlehem...was overshadowed by a grove of Tammuz, that is of Adonis. In the very cave where the infant Christ had uttered His earliest cry, lamentation was made for the lover of

Venus." (The word *katalemna,* or cave, is the one used in the gospels, thus Saint Jerome's reference to Jesus' being born in a cave, not a manger.) He adds, rather guilelessly, that it was the same cave in which Adonis was born, thus identifying Jesus with an earlier dying-and-rising god who was also connected with bread. Later, of course, Jesus would say that bread was his body. Additionally, the magi are described as following a star to find Jesus, bringing with them gifts of frankincense and myrrh. The magi were a cult that worshipped the Persian god Mithra, a solar deity whose birthday was December 25 and whose rituals, as we shall see, were closely associated with the Jesus story. The mother of Adonis, Myrrha, was cursed by the goddess Aphrodite and turned into a myrrh tree. The magi's gift of myrrh to Jesus is also a sacrifice in the Adonis cult, and its presence in the Jesus nativity suggests that the two stories have been combined.

We think of the Jews as being entirely devoted to their one god, first called El, then Yahweh, then Jehovah. However, there was also worship of other deities, most particularly the sun. As Ezekiel says, "...at the door of the temple of the Lord, between the porch and the altar, were about twenty-five men, with their backs to the temple of the Lord, and their faces toward the east, worshiping the sun toward the east." (Ezek 8:16) The connection in the gospels between Jesus, the solar deities of the era and light in some sort of conscious form, is intricate and suggestive of a level of the Jesus story that was completely buried by doctrine, specifically the doctrine that was established in the First Council of Nicea in 325 A.D. It is also suggestive that there are significant properties of the human body that we have not yet understood, but which, when they are put to use, will change the meaning of human life, in the process revolutionizing our world completely and forever.

There are many parallels between Jesus and the god-men of the polytheistic traditions, and, even if Joseph and Mary never

went there at all, the move of the birthplace of Jesus to Bethlehem may have been an attempt to replace the Adonis cult
with the new Jesus cult.

At the time the gospels were written the story of Jesus's
resurrection was spreading, not as a myth like the stories of the
other god-men who had been killed and returned to life, but as
an actual event. This inspired a strong motive to push Adonis
deeper into the cave so that Jesus could occupy it. The result is
that the Adonis story was used as the basis for a new Jesus
story. Adonis's birth was also greeted by shepherds, and his
coming was hailed by identification with a star (that of
Aphrodite, his mother, who was the Roman Venus.)

Understand, I do not think that this was done because of
some mysterious urge to replace Adonis with Jesus, but rather
because the story that Jesus's resurrection was not a myth but
an actual event was setting on fire with zeal the people who
came into contact with the apostles who were proclaiming it,
and this included the gospel authors.

Nevertheless, if Jesus was a real person, and I think that
there is more than enough evidence to support that, then the
stronger possibility is that he was from Nazareth, a poor child
and a social reject, but, as will be seen, a person of truly exceptional brilliance and unexpected and difficult to understand
powers, which collectively suggest that we have vastly underes-
timated the potential of the human being to act beyond what
appear to be the established laws of nature.

I think that the Bethlehem story is there to empower him
and make sense of his remarkable afterlife by connecting him
to the House of David, and also to suppress the Adonis cult that
was established in Bethlehem.

The Romans took pains to make sure that he died the most
humiliating death possible. They would normally have executed
a royal person who had plotted against them by beheading, not

in this way. The message was clear: this is a man who not only tried to foment an insurrection but also pretended to royal status, and who is therefore being subjected to extreme humiliation because he committed two grotesque crimes, not just one.

In view of this, the reverence given this supposed debased criminal after his execution was more than unusual, it was extraordinary. Incredibly, Joseph of Arimathea, a wealthy member of the Pharisee class—which, on the surface at least, was the enemy of Jesus—was, according to all four of the canonical gospels, the man who took responsibility for his burial.

The strange thing is that anybody did this at all. The Romans normally left executed criminals to rot on their crosses, and the mount of Golgotha was dotted with dangling corpses being slowly devoured by vermin. If Jesus was nothing more than a peasant rabble rouser, why would Pilate, who was obsessed with making examples of rebels, consent to the removal of the body and why would it have been placed in a costly tomb and apparently wrapped in an unusually fine shroud? The others that have been found have all been cotton. The Turin Shroud is linen with a herringbone weave, a luxury item. So if it was indeed the burial cloth of Jesus, there was something very unusual about him.

If Jesus was not actually a royal person, he was certainly reverenced by some powerful elements in the Jewish community.

There are three ways to look at the birth of Jesus. First, there is the suggestion that he was born in Nazareth and out of wedlock. Second, that he was born in Bethlehem because Joseph had become a refugee from unrest in Galilee or perhaps to save his betrothed from charges of adultery. Third, that he was believed by rebellious elements among the Jewish upper classes to be the actual heir to the Jewish kingdom, and Mary was taken to Bethlehem so that the birth would take place in the traditional seat of the royal family.

There is no way to make a final decision about any of this, but two final decisions have been made anyway. Traditional religious scholars believe that Jesus was born the child of a humble carpenter in Bethlehem. Secular academics believe that he was born in Nazareth, possibly of an unwed mother.

I choose to leave the various lines of speculation open—all of them, not just the ones that seem most plausible. For example, the idea that he really was recognized as the Jewish king seems to be an insupportable speculation—that is, until you look carefully at the evidence. Certain odd events that may have followed his birth (the flight into Egypt) and that happened after his death (the great care given his body) make sense if he actually was the heir to the ancient throne of David.

This also fits the gospel stories, the reason being that they were gathered out of oral tradition, and the stories that were being told about him during his life might have been intentional fictionalizations designed to obscure his true patrimony. The son of a carpenter, not a highly educated man of royal blood. Poor, not rich. Ignorant and yet brilliantly informed about Torah. All put about to protect the young king and firebrand from the Romans.

However, prophecies of the messiah predict a birth in Bethlehem and no matter where he was born and lived, these would have been codified in gospels intended to support his messianic status. After his death, his life story would have been retold to include evidence of divinity, so that the Jewish king could compete with Augustus, the deified Roman emperor whose statue was erected for worship in temples all across the empire. After the destruction of Jerusalem and the temple, these stories would have been embellished even further, to provide the Jewish diaspora with a means of maintaining their religious identity and with it their political and racial cohesion. And indeed, the writing of the gospels does coincide with the destruction of the Jewish state. Mark was written around 70 A.D., the year of the siege of Jerusalem. Except for John, which didn't reach its final form until around 100 A.D., the other canonical gospels followed over the next few years.

John's late appearance was because it was written in part to refute the Sayings Gospel of Thomas, which does not agree with the canonical gospels that Jesus was a divine being, but sees him as a man touched by God. The controversy over this distinction would eventually come close to tearing the Jesus movement apart, and would only be resolved when the power of the Roman emperor was applied on behalf of the idea that Jesus was an aspect of god, not a human being.

This book questions that decision, but not in the same way that it was questioned in ancient times. What I seek to do here is to reconceive the mystery of Jesus entirely, not to dismiss it or secularize it into another version of ordinary reality. There was very little about the life and afterlife of Jesus that could be considered ordinary.

Any biography of him that addresses all the source material available must be riddled with contradictions and unsolvable mysteries. Among those mysteries is why, if the gospel narratives were intended to prove his divinity, do the few stories we have of his childhood depict him as so bizarre? The child Jesus who emerges from the Infancy Gospel of Thomas is more demonic than divine. In fact, the book was rejected as heresy not because it was inconsistent with the four canonical gospels, which hardly mention his childhood, but because it portrayed the young Jesus as something of a monster.

There was more to it than that, though, for the Infancy Gospel is not simply a testament to the pranks of an unpleasant little boy too powerful for his own good, it is a profoundly human document—fiction or not—about a very extraordinary child's difficult coming of age. As such, it is unique not just in the Jesus material, but in the literature of the classical era, which deals hardly at all with children and childhood, let alone explores in any way the inner life and psychological struggle of a child.

It is to this remarkable and yet generally discounted document that we will now turn.

3

A STRANGE AND FRIGHTENING CHILD

The Infancy Gospel portrays an arrogant, easily angered child with bizarre magical powers which, at least at first, he abuses with complete indifference to the lives and suffering of others. As ridiculous as the stories sound to us now, in that superstitious and uninformed age many people would have seen no reason not to believe them. It was universally accepted that deities might use their divine powers in bizarre and harmful ways. After all, the stories of the Roman and Greek gods were litanies of jealousy, neurosis and familial dysfunction on a supernatural scale. And Yahweh, who turned Lot's wife into a pillar of salt and teased poor Job, was no angel, either.

The Graeco-Roman gods were a gaggle of neurotics armed with superpowers and a definite bias toward punishing upstart humans, usually quite cruelly. For the sin of giving mankind fire, the Titan Prometheus was condemned by Zeus to have his liver eaten by an eagle, and for this to be done daily in perpetuity. The god Poseidon, who found Ulysses tiresome, proceeded to play all sorts of monstrous pranks on him as he attempted to return home to Greece after fighting in the Trojan War.

There were many more such stories which were generally known in the Roman world, so the idea that a divine child might be cranky and obstreperous would have come as no surprise.

The Jews also wouldn't have been surprised that Jesus was difficult, even less so that he had strange powers. Second Kings 2: 23-25 relates what happened to some unfortunates who angered God by mocking Elisha: "From there Elisha went up to Bethel. As he was walking along the road, some boys came out of the town and jeered at him. 'Get out of here, baldy!' they said. 'Get out of here, baldy!' He turned around, looked at them and called down a curse on them in the name of the Lord. Then two bears came out of the woods and mauled forty-two of the boys. And he went on to Mount Carmel and from there returned to Samaria."

Knowing that God the Father was willing to use his powers to take over a couple of bears and turn them into killing machines that were somehow capable of mauling a remarkable forty-two boys before any of them could run off, would make it easy to believe that his son might also abuse his powers. After all, he would only be following in his father's footsteps, would he not?

There is more to it, though. If you remove the magical powers, what appears is a portrait of a brilliant and frustrated little boy trying to make his way in a world that does not understand him well at all. So these could be simply family stories, with the magical powers added later to make Jesus appear divine.

Luke, writing around 80 A.D., tells the story of Jesus questioning the scholars in the temple, a story which is also present in the Infancy Gospel. This does not necessarily mean that the entire infancy narrative dates from that time, but the Infancy temple story must be drawn from the same oral tradition that Luke drew on.

This is the only infancy story that is present in the canonical gospels because it is the only one that portrays Jesus as something other than a weird, bullying rapscallion. He is seen to be brilliant and already loyal to his mission and his heavenly father. Although only twelve, he can question the learned men so skillfully that he amazes them. Left out is any record of the difficult path from age five to age twelve, but a reading of the infancy stories reveals that, while Jesus starts out as a brat, and a markedly dangerous one, by the time he goes to the temple to question the scholars he has become a decent enough child, although so fixed on his purpose in life that he is willing to terrify his parents by leaving them without a word in order to connect with the temple scholars.

When, after days of frantic searching, they find him, they ask him why he left them without a word. He doesn't offer an apology or even regret the terror he has caused them, but instead says, "Didn't you know I had to be in my father's house?" Not very sensitive to his parents' needs, but a definite improvement over what had come before.

How could he ask questions that would amaze the scholars if he was not already educated in Torah? Of course, this quibble can be dismissed with the claim that he was divine and therefore already understood Torah perfectly. But that leads to another and actually quite crucial question, which is, if he had divine understanding, why was he asking questions at all? Both Luke and the Infancy Gospel are very specific: he was asking questions that were so brilliant that they were amazing the scholars.

The story, meant to support his divinity, actually suggests his humanity. If he was a genius child, he would ask genius questions. If he was a divinity, he would not need to ask any at all.

His extraordinary intelligence is suggested by another of the infancy stories, which brings to the surface one of the inner meanings that underly the whole of his teaching. In Infancy 6, Joseph enlists a scholar called Zacchaeus to teach Jesus the alphabet.

Jesus is about five, and Joseph has decided that it is time for him to learn his letters. Zacchaeus proceeds to recite the alphabet to Jesus, and immediately gets a surprise. Jesus announces, "Thou that knowest not the Alpha according to its nature, how canst thou teach others the Beta?" The story continues, "In the hearing of many the young child saith to Zacchaeus, Hear, O teacher, the ordinance of the first letter and pay heed to this, how that it hath lines and a middle mark, which thou seest, common to both, going apart; coming together, raised up on high, balanced of three signs, equal in measure."

In all the manuscripts we have, according to M. R. James in *The Apocryphal New Testament,* the description of the letter has been rendered "unintelligible"—that is, altered or obscured. This is likely because it is a description is of the Hebrew letter Aleph—to be precise, a form of it that appears in the Dead Sea Scrolls and dates from the first century—and not the Greek Alpha, which Greek speakers working from oral tradition would have understood as the correct description.

Like Egyptian hieroglyphics, the Hebrew letters are rich with sacred meaning, in a way that later alphabets, such as Greek, are not. The description Jesus gives of the letter: "it hath lines and a middle mark...balanced of three signs, equal in measure" expresses the ancient idea of three forces, one active, one passive, and the third balancing. It is the principle behind the Christian Trinity. It is also the foundation of the most ancient secret of the Sphinx, and so must be very old. In our era, we have come to understand that the nuclei of atoms are made up of protons and neutrons balanced and bound together by the strong force, which is why Buckminster Fuller called the triad "the building block of the universe."

The ancient concept mirrors this. In the Trinity, the Holy Spirit balances the other two forces with transcendent understanding. The active force is Jesus, taking his teaching into the world. The passive force is God, waiting to receive those who have responded to the call to "come and follow me."

In the Sphinx, the passive force is the strength of the bull, the active the courage of the lion, and the third force, balancing the other two, is the intelligence of the man.

As there is some evidence that the Sphinx at Giza could be at least 10,000 years old, it may be that this is the oldest known philosophical principle developed by the human mind, somehow expressing at one time both the foundation of inner search and the fundamental building block of the universe that was only discovered in the twentieth century—unless, of course, it was known in the deep past but lost.

The principle was well known in the time of Jesus, and expressed with elegant simplicity in this brief infancy story. But did little five-year-old Jesus actually say these words? We can think that the subtle knowledge hidden behind them was not understood by those who had control of the manuscripts, else there would have been no attempt to alter them to make the description of the letter a better fit with the Greek Alpha.

In Hebrew, Aleph means "ox" and represents strength, as does the bull in the Sphinx and God himself in the Holy Trinity. The stories illustrate the child Jesus gaining control over the power of his emotions (expressed as magical powers) and, in the last story, discovering his own compassion as he brings a dead child back to life to relieve the mother's grief.

In the first story, little Jesus, just having been brought to Egypt, upsets the local neighborhood by bringing a salted fish back to life. The family's landlady, understandably terrified of this weird child, throws them out of her house.

There follow fourteen more stories, over which Jesus gradually discovers himself as a more complex person. He goes from being a self-centered child to one curious about other people, and finally reaches a state of awareness of their vulnerabilities and needs.

Like many of the Jesus stories, the first event the infancy gospel records involves food and, in particular, fish. It prefigures his eventual identification as the leader of a group of "fishers of men." His birth took place as the astrological Age of the Fish was just beginning. The precessional calendar was moving into Pisces as the Age of Aires ended. The great precession it measures is the 25,920 years it takes for the earth's tilted axis to circle the celestial pole. It is divided into twelve 2,160 year cycles, each named for the constellation that rises before dawn on the vernal equinox during its period.

Just as the ram and sheep—Aires—are the most often mentioned animals in the Old Testament, the fish is the one most often mentioned in the New.

Whether or not this is due to knowledge of the precession is unknown, but, as it was almost certainly known to Babylonian and Egyptian astronomers, whose very ancient and long-lived civilizations had the continuity of observation needed to record the small changes that it causes, it was probably known to the Jews and Greeks who wrote the gospels as well. Aristotle certainly understood it, as it is described in detail in his *History of Animals, Book 2,* written around 320 B.C.

Jesus's boyhood troubles in Egypt did not end with the reanimation of the salted fish. Presumably, the family found another house, because the next story has Jesus walking through the city's market-place with his mother when twelve sparrows fall from a wall into the lap of a teacher who was instructing a group of boys. This makes Jesus laugh, which angers the master, who demands to know what's so funny. Jesus explains that the birds had been quarreling because they were after some corn he had in his hand. Once again a master is insulted and once again, Jesus and his long-suffering mother are thrown out, this time from the city itself. Of course, the twelve sparrows are his future twelve apostles, and the corn is the food of Jesus's teaching.

There is a prefiguring in this story involving the number 12. The number is found 187 times in the Bible. There are also twelve apostles, and the construction of the New Jerusalem in the book of Revelation involves the use of a 3-4-5 triangle, the sum of whose sides adds up to 12.

Geometry and number play a rich and complex role in the Jesus teaching, as they do in much ancient religious literature. Whether Jesus actually taught this way, or whether it comes as an overlay imposed by the gospel writers cannot be known. But, as I have mentioned previously, from earliest times, mankind has sought to create a relationship between the heavens and the earth. The New Jerusalem as it is described by John, is conceived of as an earthly reflection of the heavens. This attempt to relate heaven to earth is also at the core of Egyptian religion, and was so universal that it may even be seen in the skyward journey of souls depicted in the 2,000-year-old White Shaman petroglyph in South Texas. While archaeologists consider the message of the White Shaman to be incomprehensible, there seems to be a connection between the petroglyph and the ancient idea of a path to the stars. The shaman appears to be directing souls upward toward a river of stars. The nearby Pecos River, where it widens out just south of the location of the White Shaman cave, would have seasonally reflected the Milky Way just as the Nile did. Sitting on the bluff overlooking the Lower Pecos of an evening, I have seen this magnificent sight.

The Egyptians believed that souls returned to the stars from the point where the reflection of Milky Way touched the Nile. Was the belief present also among the unknown people who created the White Shaman? Without a written record, we cannot know, but it would seem so.

Eusebius (260—340 A.D.), who authored an early story of the church called *Ecclesiastical History*, described the infancy stories as fiction. However, as Jesus would hardly have been the only genius child who has proved temperamental, controlling and strange, to me they read more like embellished family stories.

If you look past the miracles, a portrait emerges of a brilliant and impetuous little boy. Across the fifteen stories, his character develops and matures. In its sensitivity to character, the Infancy Gospel is unique in the skimpy ancient literature of the child.

In the first of the stories, he is found on the Sabbath making clay sparrows in some little pools of water he has created near a brook. People complain to his father that he is violating the Sabbath. He claps his hands, causing the clay sparrows to come to life and fly away. The son of a scribe then uses a branch to open up the pools, causing the water to run out. Jesus does not take this well and says, "Thou shalt be withered like a tree." He goes home, but the parents of the withered boy follow and demand that he be "restored." The story ends there. Presumably the unfortunate child remained withered. If there is truth behind the story, it could be that Jesus, helpless to prevent the child of a man higher on the social ladder from ruining his play, threatened him in some way.

The next misdeed involves Jesus being touched, something to which he is also recorded elsewhere as being sensitive. In Infancy 5, Jesus is walking in Nazareth with Joseph when a boy strikes him on the arm. Jesus retaliates by causing him to drop dead. (One can believe that he yelled something at him along the lines of "Drop dead," and was hurried away by his father.) People are upset and when some of them speak ill of him, he strikes them blind. Joseph then shakes him by the ear—which is, as is true of most of the other stories, an entirely inappropriate response, given the damage Jesus has done. However, if the miracle is taken out of the narrative, then Joseph's response makes sense. His son threatens somebody and he shakes him by the ear.

When Joseph touches him, Jesus reacts in an unusual way. He says, "It sufficeth thee to see me and not to touch me." To me, this suggests that he understood perfectly well that his father was capable of striking him and he was bargaining for deliverance from a blow. Perhaps he was also uneasy about being touched. Hypervigilance accompanies such phobias, and when concern with touch appears again in Mark 5: 30—34, Jesus does seem to display a hypervigilant response. When a woman touches his cloak, he is instantly aware and turns to her, asking "Who has touched my clothes?" The woman, who had been cured by him of protracted menstrual bleeding, "came and fell down before him and told him all the truth." He uttered a line that has resonated through the ages, "Thy faith hath made thee whole."

Phobic and hypervigilant he might have been, but the words and actions of Jesus also reveal, in many cases, not just more than normal empathy, but extraordinary empathy, and, as will be seen, there may have been more to his awareness of touch than a simple phobia.

In Infancy 7, Jesus is said to have accidentally been involved in another boy's falling off a roof and dying. But he was not angry with him, and therefore brought him back to life—a first for him, and a sign that the author of the stories wished to express the idea that, as he grew up, his personality was evolving.

Then comes Infancy 8, where Jesus heals the foot of a boy and, for the first time, is called a god by observers.

This is the first of what will become a substantial collection of healing stories, which will fill both the canonical gospels and apocryphal stories.

Stories 9, 10 and 11 involve Jesus doing more miraculous

deeds, but then in Story 12 there is a setback. Jesus is now eight years old, and once again, Joseph attempts to find him a teacher. But Jesus thinks this teacher even more of an idiot than Zacchaeus, and ends up striking him dead.

Mary and Joseph must have been close to the end of their tether because Joseph tells her to no longer let him leave the house. In the "real" version of this story, one can infer that his frustration with having to endure another teacher who was not as intelligent as he was may have caused him to physically attack this man. Given all of the times in the stories that he strikes people dead or blind or transforms them in upsetting ways, say, into goats, he may well have lived in a state of great frustration and as a result had a short temper and an inclination to violence.

Things went a bit better with the next teacher, largely because Joseph plots with the man, who promises to be "gentle." In ancient times, teachers beat their students as the primary means of discipline. Not a good idea with Jesus, as Joseph now very clearly realizes. Prefiguring the temple story, Jesus enters the teacher's house, sees a book, opens it and, instead of reading from it, teaches the professor so brilliantly that he becomes the student. The boy, who had been maddened by one dullard teacher after another, must have been delighted. They get on well, and Jesus says, "For thy sake shall he rise again who was dead."

The fact that he says this to a teacher who has been willing to question his own knowledge suggests that the teaching Jesus is evolving in his own mind is about finding one's own inner path to understanding. As will be seen when we discuss the Thomas Sayings Gospel, Jesus did not wish to instruct, but rather to facilitate students in finding their own inner way. Who rises again, here, is the soul that had been asleep to its own inner life.

The Infancy Gospel is intended to convince the reader that

Jesus is more than a brilliant child struggling to control a powerful mind and an intense personality, but rather is a divine being learning to control his powers.

In the last two stories, Jesus is a very different child at eleven and twelve than he was a five. In Story 14, he does his brother James a great good turn when James is bitten by a snake. Jesus breathes on the wound and saves his life. James, who had been uneasy about his brother during Jesus's lifetime, became one of the first apostles and after his crucifixion, brought the message of him as messiah into the Jewish community.

The fifteenth and last of the infancy stories concerns a neighbor child who died and is brought back to life by Jesus. This was apparently an infant, as Jesus next tells the mother to "take up thy child and give him suck, and remember me."

Jesus has now developed empathy and control over his powers, and the Infancy Gospel ends.

One can imagine Jesus frantically sucking venom out of a snakebite and saving James's life, or flaring up when the child struck him on the arm. In fact, his difficult relations with other children, when all the claims of wonder-working are removed, read as stories from the life of a headstrong and precocious little boy who was often teased by other children, to the point that he would lash out violently at them.

If he had been born out of wedlock and was living in a small town like Nazareth, he would have been bullied, which, for a sensitive and brilliant child would have been particularly awful, and might well have set up in him a lifelong desire to both keep his origins secret and even to put himself forth as someone who was more than an ordinary human being.

The continual references to teachers also suggest that Joseph was something other than a *tekton*. A carpenter would not have had any reason to want his children to learn to read, let alone the wherewithal to hire teachers. If indeed the family lived in Nazareth, we know from the archaeological evidence that they must have been poor. You are not going to be able to hire a teacher with a bronze farthing, if you could even get one to come out of one of the cities to a little hamlet like that.

On the other hand, if this was a royal or noble family living in Bethlehem, once you strip away the miracles, the stories make logical sense.

However, if Jesus was a carpenter's son but so precocious that he went on his own to the temple and began to dialog with the priests and scribes and impressed them sufficiently, then in Jewish culture, with its respect for learning, he might conceivably have been given an education.

If he was a royal child, though, then his brilliance would have been carefully nurtured, and the teacher and temple stories may reflect that. A royal child might treat teachers he considered incompetent very much as arrogant little Jesus did. But once his life entered oral tradition, the secret of his royal birth might have needed to have been even more deeply hidden. This would explain the general insistence on his birth as a carpenter's son or, in the case of Mark, as a fatherless child. The reason for this would have been that, as he had been executed for sedition, had the Romans been certain that his really was a royal family, its surviving members would have been in jeopardy and along with them the entire Jesus movement. In the years after his execution, the movement was run by James and the other apostles almost as an underground organization, exactly as it would have been had it been part of the growing Jewish independence movement.

As matters stood, Jesus followers Peter, Andrew, Paul, James the brother of Jesus, Thaddaeus, Matthew, Bartholomew, Simon the Zealot, James the Apostle, James the Less and probably others lost to history were all executed, some by the Jews for blasphemy and others by the Romans. As the Romans practiced religious tolerance (they had to, or they would have had to depopulate their empire), they would not have been imposing the death penalty for religious reasons. The ones executed by them must all have been regarded as political criminals. It would have been a dangerous matter to go about their empire preaching the message of an executed king who had expressed hostility toward the Romans.

Like Luke, which is the only other gospel that contains the temple story, the Infancy Gospel was probably written around 80 A.D. This would mean that the miracles Jesus had performed during his adult life would have been known to the author, which is probably what inspired him to add miracles to the family stories. If Jesus had been a miracle-working divine being in adulthood, he must have been one as a child, too, so the author would have assumed that, even if the specific miracles he names did not happen, because miracles occurred when he was an adult, they certainly did during his childhood, too.

Like the gospels and the apocrypha, the text is a *bios*, or biography, which in ancient times was a document intended to support the reputation of its subject, not necessarily be a factual account of the person's life.

But what about those adult miracles? Did he heal the sick, calm storms, raise the dead?

There were other miracle workers in the ancient world, but the stories about the strange man that was Jesus stand out both for their number and the many witnesses involved, and the persistence of those witnesses in continuing to proclaim them even after the Romans had executed him.

Unless there was something exceptionally convincing about the stories, it seems unlikely that they would do that—let alone risk their lives to proclaim his resurrection.

Were there miracles, then? Really?

4

THE WHISPERING SERPENT AND THE MAGICIAN

The oldest site that we have any certain reason to think of as religious is found in a cave in the Tsodilo Hills in Botswana, a region known as the Louvre of the Desert because of the magnificent and numerous rock carvings and paintings that have been created throughout the area.

The cave itself contains a natural formation shaped like a snake, which has been carved with scales and eyes that seem to come to life at night when flickering light shines on them. From a chamber behind the cave wall, the slightest whisper fills the cave with an eerie, disembodied voice.

Seventy thousand years ago, hunters seem to have come here for guidance, for there have been excavated from beneath the cave floor hundreds of broken spear points, apparently sacrificed in order to gain help from the serpent god.

The oldest religious site in the world thus enshrines one of our deepest and most intensely felt archetypes, that of the serpent, and is also a place of magic and illusion, where people went in search of help from the gods.

In that cave, you can almost hear the voice that once whispered from the hidden chamber behind the carving, and you think to yourself of the serpent of the spine in Egyptian soul-magic, demonized in Genesis, removed from the body and left lurking in a tree; of Apollo in his serpent form, a magical, winged phallus; and of the pythoness at Delphi in Greece, who would inhale the hypnotizing breath of the underworld, then prophesy.

Religion is about using magical ritual to induce deities to apply their powers on our behalf. Science is about using technical ritual to control the powers of nature.

This, incidentally, is why the culture of science and the culture of religion, with their parallel revealed truths, heresies, apostasies and miracles function socially in such similar ways. Both are ruled by believers, reject apostates and banish heretics.

Like religious miracles, scientific miracles require careful preparation and strict adherence to certain processes if they are to work. The difference, of course, is that the scientific operations will, if correctly carried out, consistently produce an expected result. When religious miracles transpire, say, after prayer or the laying on of hands, they cannot be explained, at least not in the same way that scientific operations can. They are never consistently repeatable.

They do happen, though. The impossible is not entirely that.

As scientific knowledge began to expand in the eighteenth century, science based on theory and experiment came to seem a better way of gaining positive results when trying to influence nature than prayer or magic. By the end of the century, the old methods were losing their credibility, and many people were starting to think that the religious promise was a fraud. People became conflicted over what to do about the fact that science usually worked and religion usually didn't. If prayer was irrelevant and God an imaginary being, then what of morals? Why not simply live by greed, and let the weak die?

While this very approach, led by evangelists such as Ayn Rand, is rapidly becoming the signature of modern post-moral civilization, it bothered many intellectuals of the era, and they set out to find ways of preserving the morality that had emerged with Christianity while at the same time seeing Jesus as human, not divine, and the miracles and resurrection as hyperbole.

But without his divinity, where would his moral authority come from?

Thomas Jefferson completed *The Life and Morals of Jesus of Nazareth,* commonly known as The Jefferson Bible, in 1820. It is not an original work, but was constructed by cutting and pasting sections of the New Testament. It removes all mention of the miracles and the resurrection, leaving only the life story and the teachings. It is, in effect, a secular gospel. He regarded it as a private document and never published it, but did show it to friends. In a letter to John Adams in 1813, he described it as being "for my own use."

Reading it, it is clear that what he wanted to preserve were the moral precepts and the teachings about the rights of man, and remove stories that underpin the claim that Jesus was a divine being. But privately. Allowing his heretical personal conviction to become public knowledge would, in those days, have been extremely inconvenient, and not only politically. Among some of his close friends, there would have been a very negative reaction.

In 1835, David Freidrich Strauss published *The Life of Jesus,* which argued that the miracles, the resurrection, and, in fact, much of the New Testament, are all myth. This is now accepted in almost all academic circles as the truth: the miracles almost certainly did not happen, and the resurrection certainly didn't.

I think that many of the miracles not only happened, but that they can be understood. As to the resurrection, as I have suggested and as will be seen in more detail when we address it in later chapters, there is startling new evidence that something extremely unusual may indeed have taken place after Jesus's crucifixion. If so, it didn't necessarily prove his divinity, but it did serve notice to us that we don't fully understand our humanity. Indeed, as will be seen, there may be things about us —powers—that the decision to take Jesus as an aspect of god has concealed from us.

In ancient times, magic was almost universally believed to be real. Intellectuals would scoff, but not the common people. Its power was so feared that its use was held to be illegal in most ancient states. Famously, in the Bible, there occurs the admonition, "Do not allow a sorceress to live." (Exodus 22:18) It is prohibited in the Twelve Tables, the earliest Roman legal document, and the Cornelian Law on Assassins and Poisoners, adopted in 81 B.C., was the statute under which magicians were generally prosecuted. In Latin, the word *veneficus* was used interchangeably to mean poisoner and magician, and the practice of magic remained illegal throughout the Roman period. The most severe penalties were applied, including being fed to animals in the arena, crucifixion, and being burned alive.

While Pilate condemned Jesus for sedition, he also may have done it for magical practice. In Matthew 27:63, the Jewish officials tell Pilate that Jesus, "that deceiver," has said that he would rise again on the third day after his death. The use of the word "deceiver" is a possible reference to magic, as magicians were commonly referred to as "deceivers." Justin Martyr, writing in the second century, comments that Jesus had a reputation as an illusionist, which, under Roman law, was also recognized as a form of illegal magical practice.

Illegality did not stop people from calling on sorcerers, tricksters and astrologers of every sort all over the empire, and the archeological record is full of amulets, bowls and many other objects connected with magic.

In the *Didache*, a first century document that outlines the

Christian way of life, it is specifically prohibited in Commandment Two: "You shall not commit murder, you shall not commit adultery, you shall not commit pederasty, you shall not commit fornication, you shall not steal, you shall not practice magic, you shall not practice witchcraft, you shall not murder a child by abortion nor kill that which is born." (Lest the prohibition against the killing of living infants seems unnecessary, it should be remembered that exposure of unwanted babies was legal in the Roman Empire at the time the *Didache* was composed.)

Any miracle worker would certainly have been considered a practitioner of magic. The idea that Jesus's magic was special because he was divine did not appear until later.

In the part of the empire that included Palestine, there were two kinds of magician, the *goes* and the *magos*. The *goetes* were associated with what we would now call shamanism and, when they cast spells designed to harm the victim, black magic.

The Jews of first century Palestine were a colonized and oppressed people, entirely powerless against their Roman masters. The only thing they had that offered them any sense of control over their own lives was magic, so you can be sure that there were many *goetes* and *magi* in the region, and, illegal or not, that they had busy practices.

In the canonical gospels, Jesus's magical practice is essentially that of the *goetes*. He sought to free people from physical afflictions, to relieve the anguish of insanity, and, above all, to feed them. This last was particularly important, because, in those days in Palestine, everyone below the propertied classes was at least somewhat hungry much of the time. The farmers, for example, could only stand and watch as the tax collectors carried away food they needed for their families. And then there was the unpredictable weather, always a problem in the region even during that period, which is known as the Roman Climate Optimum because of its generally stable weather, but areas on the southern fringe of the empire remained vulnerable to drought. So between the Romans and the weather, for the people of places like Palestine semi-starvation was an ordinary part of life, and famine a constant threat.

Spells and prayer were what the common man had to try to protect himself and relieve his suffering. He might not be able to stop the tax collector, but he could hire a *goetes* to cast a spell against him.

Magic and religion were until very recently so intimately linked that they may be called interdependent cultural forces. Even now, when a Catholic priest blesses the water and wine during mass, he is enacting a magical spell. If he is Anglican or Episcopal, he believes that this act is symbolic. A Roman Catholic believes that the actual, living presence of Jesus as Christ enters the water and wine as he utters his formula. In other words, he carries out a magic ritual that has a supernatural result. In fact, the first words of the ritual in the Tridentine Mass, "hoc est corpus" gave to the expanding secular culture in the sixteenth century the magician's words of power, "hocus-pocus."

The earliest reference to Jesus as Christ appears on a bowl dating from the first century A.D., which was found by French archaeologists in Egypt during an underwater dig in the harbor of Alexandria. Etched on it is the inscription *"Dia Christou O Goistais,"* or "By Christ the Magician." There is no way to be certain that it is a reference to Jesus, but two of the earliest representations of the crucifixion, dating from a hundred years later, are found on magical amulets. A brown jasper from around 200 A.D. is carved with the image of Jesus dangling from his cross. The inscription on it invokes Jesus, then continues on with a coded magical incantation. Another jasper, this one yellow, depicts the crucified Jesus on one side and is covered with magical symbols on the other.

In his treatise against Christianity, Celsus says of Jesus, "Is it not also true that you hired yourself out as a workman in Egypt where you learned magic-making, and by this means gained something of a name for yourself which you now flaunt among your kinsmen?"

In Mark 8:22—26, Jesus heals a blind man by spitting on his eyes. There are many examples in ancient magical texts of medical spitting, and one way it was used was to cure weak vision. The cure applied by Jesus in Mark involves a man who has been totally blind, and requires two applications of spittle. After the first, the man can see, but people look "like trees walking around." The initial application of the magic brings the man from no vision at all to nearsightedness. Then there is a second touching of the eyes, after which "he saw everything clearly." A formal double application of the spell to reach full efficacy was also a common part of magical ritual in the era.

Spitting is recorded in Egyptian magic in many different texts, including the Book of the Dead, where the first mention of it occurs. Spell 17 of that text reads in part, "...when his eye was sick from weeping...then Thoth would spit on it." This records one of the most famous healings in Egyptian myth, and became the basis for the use of spittle in the magical arts, suggesting that Jesus did indeed learn his craft in Egypt.

Spitting is also mentioned in Jewish magical texts, and the Roman physicians Galen and Celsus (not the anti-Christian author) both mention its curative properties. (Galen, *On the Natural Faculties*, III and IV, and Celsus *On Medicine*, V).

In Jesus's time, magic and medicine were so interconnected that they may be said to be two aspects of the way the ancients conceived of healing. However, his admonitions in the canonical gospels, especially in the earliest one (Mark) that his healing must be kept secret is a stronger indication that he was practicing magic of a kind that was viewed as illegal.

Magical texts from the period, such as the Greek Magical Papyri, counsel secrecy as a way of preserving the power of ritual. This was well known in ancient times, which is likely one reason that most of the requests for secrecy appear only in the earliest gospel. Matthew and Luke, perhaps seeing that Jesus's demands for secrecy that appear throughout Mark suggest that he was practicing illegal magic, removed them.

As the movement spread after Jesus's crucifixion, "secret" gospels proliferated, but none of these save the Sayings Gospel of Thomas appear to be particularly early texts. Thomas may have been written between the 60s and the 70s, the same decade in which Mark was created—and indeed, it doesn't just make frequent references to secrecy throughout, its prologue identifies it as a list of secret teachings and sayings. There are also many connections between Thomas and Mark. Certainly, both authors worked from the same oral sources, as we shall see when we explore Thomas.

The Romans appear to have thought that Jesus's followers practiced magic. When Pliny the Younger, in his famous 112 A.D. letter to Trajan about a group of Christians brought before him for practicing strange rituals, speaks of their "depraved and extravagant superstitions," he is most likely referring to what he would have regarded as magical practice.

In Roman law, magicians were referred to in a number of ways, among them "doers of evil" and "depraved" as well as "deceivers." Suetonius, writing around 121 A.D., comments in his biography of Nero in *The Lives of the Twelve Caesars* that "penalties were imposed on the Christians, a sort of men who practice a new superstition involving magic." This would have been the Communion ritual.

The letter says that the Christians told him that they "recite a hymn to Christ," which Pliny may have taken as an incantation, and thus illegal, but he does not state this specifically.

In his *Dialogue with Trypho*, the Christian writer Justin Martyr, also writing around the year 160, has Trypho (a fictional Jew) say that Jesus was "a Galilean magician." That Suetonius believed this and Justin felt it necessary to refute it means that it was in general circulation at that time.

It's not clear that Jesus or his followers refuted it. On the contrary, they saw Jesus's magical powers as protective. In Revelation 19:16 it is stated that "on his robe and on his thigh he has written king of king and lord of lords." Paul in Galatians 6:17 claims that marks of Jesus on his own body have magical power when he says "Let no one cause me trouble, for I bear on my body the marks of Jesus."

Egypt and Greece were the primary sources of magical knowledge at the time, but the only record of the Egyptian use of tattoos involves women. The Greeks and the Jews (also famous for their magical practices) both used tattoos to fix magical powers on the bodies of practitioners. After Greek and Jewish magicians had been trained, they commonly had symbols representing the powers they possessed tattooed onto their bodies, as Jesus did.

His teaching is obviously far more than the work, as Celsus would have it, of a commonplace magician, but as the miracles are magical acts, magical practice must have played a role in his ministry, and a very crucial one.

So what was magic in the first century A.D., how did it work (and did it work?) and how might Jesus have used it?

There are over fifty miracles recorded in the canonical gospels and many more in the Apocrypha. And, of course, there is the resurrection, the most improbable miracle of them all.

I will not be approaching the miracles either from the viewpoint of a Christian believer or a secular skeptic. As I have lived a life full of experiences that were supposedly impossible, and seen and participated in many events that could be classified as miracles, my approach obviously must be rather a different one.

Those who believe that Jesus was not strictly human, but a

divine being in human form, argue that the miracles must have worked as described; the skeptics argue that the physical miracles (food multiplications, resurrections, physical healings, etc.) are impossible.

While it is generally agreed by both sides that the exorcisms must have sometimes been at least temporarily effective in treating florid examples of insanity, I think that some of the seemingly impossible ones may have worked as well. Some could have been accomplished quite easily with sleight of hand, illusions and the use of assistants. After all, as we have seen at Tsodilo, illusions and assistants have been in use by magicians for at least 70,000 years.

What magic is, and what is called magic in one historical period or another, depends entirely on how much is known, at any given time, about how the world actually works.

Someone looking into their own future even from as recently as 1820, the year Jefferson penned his Bible, would perceive our world as almost entirely magical—light without flames, vehicles powering themselves, devices filled with people flying through the air, voices and music emanating from small boxes, recorded images both moving and still—the list would be a long one.

The farther back in history you go, the less people understand and the more mysterious the world is to them—as well, the more helpless they are and therefore the more desperate they feel in the face of the incomprehensible powers that control their lives—storms, floods, droughts, disease, the mysterious march of the seasons.

The less we understand how natural laws work, the more open we are to the possibility that magic might. The more ignorant we are, the more opportunities charlatans have to victimize us. For the same reason, though, we are also open to possibilities that knowledge will later close to us. For example, in the time of Jesus, a man suffering from schizophrenia would feel certain that he had a demon inside him, so a magician, exorcising him with sufficient authority and drama, might well succeed in suppressing his symptoms, at least for a time. Similarly, to people who believed completely in the efficacy of magic, the placebo effect could have been very powerful. Even now, it can have a dramatic effect. In the December 2020 issue of the journal *Pain*, there was a study reported by Andrea Powell and others that showed that people suffering chronic pain could be helped by a placebo cream applied to their forearms if they were told that it might or might not be a placebo. (In fact, only placebo creams were applied.)

This is just one of hundreds of studies that show that the placebo response is real. In a world that believed in magic and knew nothing of the placebo effect, it may have been more powerful than it is now, conceivably much more. It could have been an effective curative, which would explain why magicians were so much in demand despite the law.

To read the words of Jesus in the *Quelle* or "source" gospel, commonly called the Q gospel, which is a scholarly reconstruction of the text that all three synoptic gospels must have drawn on, is to find a voice that resonates with power and decision. This was a man on fire with his certainty that he belonged to God. The bedrock of his soul was the belief that he had a message from God and a direct connection to God, and close behind it that God would respond when he asked for support.

There is nothing in these early texts to suggest that he thought himself a divine being, but everything to suggest that he believed himself to be a human being chosen by God to do his work on earth.

His extraordinary level of conviction was communicated with a stirring power that leaps from the pages of *Quelle*. This conviction would have been crystal clear to anybody he met, and it is likely to be what caused his miracles to work. Thus it isn't surprising that he was mobbed with supplicants. Word would have spread far and wide about such a powerful magician. Moreover, as is pointed out in all of the synoptic gospels, he did them for free, which, in a community where many people did not have a bronze *prutah*—the proverbial "widow's mite"—at once set him apart from the horde of magic-workers who plied their trade among the desperate.

In a time when medicine was often at least as lethal as disease, someone who could activate the placebo effect would have had much higher status than a conventional doctor, who as often as not made the patient sicker or killed him outright.

When magic worked, people just assumed that the deities the magician claimed were behind it were real.

Most of our ancestors, even well into the nineteenth century, lived in a world that was governed by supernatural beings and magic. Even to this day, it's easy to find working magicians, and I don't mean stage illusionists, but people who will carry out rituals intended to cause healing or apply curses, and so forth. There are thousands upon thousands of stories of miraculous healings on the internet, attributed to the intervention of God, Jesus, and many other deities, and to professional healers. Millions of people turn to prayer every day.

Magic is now believed to depend entirely on conviction, both of the practitioner and the subject. But I don't think it's all the placebo effect.

In Jesus's magical practice, he used a combination of suggestion, sympathetic magic, and—well—the inexplicable.

Given that he lived and worked in a place and in an age where magicians, prophets and illusionists were commonplace, he must have really stood out to draw the kind of crowds that he did. He also must have had a remarkable voice. In that era, a commanding voice was essential to oratory because there were no amplification devices. And yet, when he spoke, he was capable of causing large crowds to react with awe. He must have been an exceptional speaker to do that, which in those days meant not only an ability to fill the voice with emotion, but to do it while shouting.

The accounts of the occasion that he delivered the Sermon on the Mount say that he stood on a hill before a large crowd. He must have been able to project a voice blaring loud and yet communicating the dignity and compassion in those words, or they would not have come ringing down through the ages.

That, in itself, is a form of magic, and no less magical is the amazing fact that we know of him at all. Among other things, this is because, sometime around forty years after his death, a truly striking phenomenon began to take place. We take it for granted now, but the fact that people decided to commit the stories that were circulating about him to the written word is in itself a miracle.

The Beatitudes are at once a document of great spiritual significance and, as a towering proclamation of the value of the common man, also one of the most powerful political statements on record, if not the most powerful. They are a condemnation of the slavery that defined life in the Roman Empire, and stand as the first and greatest cry for freedom that has ever been uttered.

Are the Beatitudes an act of magic, though, or a spiritual and political statement? I would argue that they are all three, and as we seek deeper into the teachings, we will see that they have, in addition to political and spiritual meaning, a significant power to reach levels of self-worth and dignity that sleep within us like giants trapped by some malign spell. In this sense, they are also magic of the most pure kind there can be, which reaches into the hidden prison within us all and unlocks its door just as surely as an earthquake once unlocked a jail into which Paul had been cast, and frees us to walk into the light.

Identifying Jesus as a magician was not negative as far as the common people were concerned. Those who heard him

speak and clamored after his miracles would have been interested only in whether or not the miracles worked, but the
upper classes who knew the law would have been uneasy. The
line between magic that was contrary to the moral order and
sacred practice was a fine one. The concern of the gospel
writers was that the miracles of Jesus might fall on the wrong
side of that line, so they were at pains to identify the miracles as
originating from Jesus's divinity and not from magical practice.
Jesus probably felt exactly the same way, which would be why
he offered his skills for free and, for the most part, in public.
Magicians worked for money. Jesus sought to identify himself
with a higher calling, and so did the gospel writers. During the
period, acceptable magic was called *theourgia,* rituals designed
to invoke deities. Then there was a middle form, *mageia,* using
ritual to cause change in the natural world. If this was done for
good purposes, such as bringing rain, it was not illegal. *Goetia*
was illegal magic, and Jesus's reputation for healings and
drawing the dead back to life placed him perilously close to
this category. Had he been doing it for money, it would have
been thought that illusion and deception were involved, and he
would have been subject to arrest.

His powers were not only inherited by some of his apostles
after his death, but apparently continued to work for many of
his devotees in years to come. And, in fact, if any of the miracles
attributed to saints, and that have happened at Lourdes and so
forth, are to be believed, they work to this day.

Paul could perform miracles, and, it would seem, quite
convincingly, as one reported in Acts 16 led to him being taken
before a magistrate, beaten despite the fact that he was a
Roman citizen, and imprisoned.

He had been preaching in Philippi in Macedonia when he
began to be followed by a slave girl who was famously
possessed, so much so that her owners made a great deal of
money from her prophesying. For days she followed along

singing his praises, until finally he became annoyed enough to perform the exorcism miracle he had learned either from direct observation of Jesus in action, or gained the conviction to perform by hearing the stories told about Jesus after his own miraculous encounter with him outside Damascus.

There is only one suggestion in Paul's writings that he may have been a direct witness to Jesus while he was alive. This occurs in 2 Corinthians 5:16. The Greek text is generally translated somewhat vaguely, but the Jerusalem Bible has a literal version: "Though we knew Jesus when he was alive, we no longer see him physically."

If this is correct, then Paul had at least been an observer during Jesus's lifetime. As his conversion did not happen until after Jesus's death, however, and as he instigated the martyrdom of Saint Stephen also after the death of Jesus, it must be assumed that, during Jesus's lifetime, if he was a witness, he was a hostile one.

In any case, he knew enough about Jesus's methods to use them to cast out demons, as he did this for the slave girl. His efforts must have been noticeably effective, as she could no longer prophesy after he was finished. This made her owners furious enough for them to haul him before the local magistrate, who had him publicly whipped and thrown into jail.

All ended well, though, thanks to the earthquake which frightened the jailer into believing in Paul's power and releasing him. When the magistrate found out that he was a Roman citizen, he apologetically escorted him out of the city—but note, he did not ask him to stay.

It was no small thing to take a person before a magistrate in the Roman Empire. The governor might send armed men or even troops in a case involving the state, but if a private person was to bring somebody to judgment, they had to do it themselves. This is why Acts records, "When her owners realized that their hope of making money was gone, they seized Paul and Silas and dragged them into the marketplace to face the authorities." (Acts 16:19)

Paul's exorcism worked so well that it ruined the owners' business.

What of the man who inspired Paul and others so profoundly that they were themselves able to do miracles? What sort of a life led from the Jesus we leave in the temple at the age of twelve, to the Jesus who comes striding back from his baptism by John sixteen years later demanding of the first people he meets, "Follow me?"

We have explored the missing years between his birth and the age of 12. Now it's time to go into the more famous of Jesus's "lost years," and see what can be deduced about what happened to him after his parents recovered him from the temple at age 12 and before he reappeared at about 28.

Where did he go? What did he do? There are stories that he went east and was influenced by Buddhism, also that Buddhist monks may have accompanied caravans along the Silk Road, and their teachings reached his ears. But, in the end, his movements have heretofore been a mystery.

Something extraordinary happened to him, though. As will be seen later, he was supported during his passion by unknown individuals who seem to have possessed some very unusual and powerful knowledge. During his lost years, was he the student of such people?

What happened to him to cause him to demand people drop everything and follow him? What made him able to perform miracles, and did they actually work?

5

JESUS EMPOWERED

There are presently two general approaches to the miracles of Jesus. The most prevalent one is that they were invented as hyperbole designed to convince potential followers of the improbable idea that a man who had spouted blasphemies and seditions and gotten himself killed for his troubles was actually an incarnated aspect of god. The other is that he was indeed god incarnate, and they are all true. Between these two extremes, there is a strain of academic scrutiny, as I have mentioned, that suggests that the exorcisms might have worked, at least somewhat.

I propose to take another approach. Rather than explore all the miracles mentioned in the canonical gospels, I will address just some of the physical miracles, the two that appear in Q and some of those in Mark.

First, though, it is important to understand a little more about the Mark gospel. It is easy to assume that, as it appears to have been the first one written, its stories must be closest to actual events in the life of Jesus. However, it contains more miracles than any of the other gospels, some of which must be illusions and others authorial inventions. I think that I can show that many of the Markian miracles probably happened, but not all.

Like the other gospels, Mark is written in relatively simple Greek. The author was not a scholar or particularly literate. It appears to be intended for a gentile audience, and was created to promote the cause of Jesus as a divinity.

In Section X, "Of Miracles" of his *Enquiry Concerning Human Understanding,* published in 1748, David Hume voices what has become the fundamental argument against the miracles. It is that they violate the order of nature and therefore cannot have happened. This has remained the argument against them ever since. Christian religionists agree that they violate nature, but say that this only proves that they were performed by somebody outside of nature—God, who created nature and therefore can deform its laws as he pleases.

I would suggest, from my own experience of life, that there are natural phenomena that we do not yet understand and thus dismiss as "supernatural" and say cannot really happen. But we would have said the same thing about heavier- than-air travel and radio just a couple of generations ago, so I am not willing to be so dismissive. I think there are ways of manipulating the physical world that Jesus either understood or activated without knowing how he did it. I don't see any reason why they can't be understood, though. I think they will be.

The Q gospel mentions two miracles. Mark, the first of the canonical gospels, records those two and fourteen more. The whole body of the canonical gospels contains a total of forty specifically described miracles, and comments that suggest many others. Jesus was not just a miracle worker, he appears to have been a startlingly prolific miracle worker.

What could have been happening was that the gospel writers kept adding miracles to the list, possibly because public skepticism was increasing as the Jesus story spread. This may also have been because, as the stories circulated among the Jews, there was resistance to the idea that Jesus had been the anointed one, the heir of David. One reason for this would have been because he was from Galilee, which was, like Idumea, a place of forced conversion. (Generations before, both regions had been conquered by Israel and the inhabitants compelled to worship Yahweh.) The Mishna describes the Galileans as having different marriage rites, different weights and measures and a distinct accent. (The Mishna dates from the third century A.D., but it was a collection of earlier oral traditions, written down to help the dispersed Jews of that period maintain cultural solidarity.) In addition to these reasons, as the grandchild of a forced convert, Jesus would have been viewed by Jews with the same suspicion with which they regarded the Idumean Herod. So when the Jesus followers came forward with their claim that this Galilean, whose religious loyalty must be suspect, was not just a Jew, but the ultimate Jew, the messiah himself and the Davidic heir, there was resistance that only grew stronger as the story spread.

Most scholars believe that the Mark gospel was written in Galilee or in Rome between 65 and 75 A.D. If it was written in Rome, then it is possible that it is both a reaction to the persecution of Christians that took place after the Great Fire of Rome in 64 A.D., and a response to the rebellion that was then unfolding in Judea. In fact, many scholars identify it as the "wartime gospel," because of its reference to the destruction of the temple in the "little apocalypse" which is recorded in Mark 13.

Tacitus reports that Nero, who was himself being blamed for the fire, scapegoated the Christians to draw suspicion away from himself. As Tacitus also states that they were "a class hated for their abominations," they would have been an easy choice. Nero had a "multitude" of them rounded up, and subjected them to bizarre and horrific public executions, including being torn apart by animals and being set alight and used as torches to illuminate gardens at night.

Among the things that probably made them seem strange was their habit of greeting each other with the sign of the Vesica Piscis. This was done by holding the hands together as if in prayer, then opening them, raising them, and closing them again. In fact, the figure in the Alexamenos graffito, which shows a worshiper with a raised hand paying homage to an image on a cross with the head of a donkey, may be making this gesture. (The graffito was discovered in ruins on the Palatine Hill in Rome and dates between 100 and 200 A.D.) As the goddess Venus was symbolized by the Vesica Piscis, the gesture would not have endeared the Christians to the Roman polytheists. Judging from Pliny's letter to Trajan, Christians were thought, probably because of communion, to be cannibals. Writing in the first half of the third century, a pro-Christian Roman lawyer called Minucius Felix, in his *Octavius*, constructed as a dialogue, has one of his characters describe this common misconception in this way: "An infant covered over with meal, that it may deceive the unwary, is placed before him who is to be stained with their rites: this infant is slain by the young pupil, who has been urged on as if to harmless blows on the surface of the meal, with dark and secret wounds. Thirstily - O horror! they lick up its blood; eagerly they divide its limbs."

The reason for such confusion was that the Christian community in Rome would have been living a radically different life from the rest of the population. While the *Didache* outlines what life in a Christian community was like by around 100 A.D., we can infer from Thessalonians 1 how they would have been living in Rome in the earlier time that Paul was writing—in fact, prior to and during the time that Mark was being written.

In 1 Thessalonians 3—8, Paul counsels against what he calls sexual immorality, which probably included sexual contact forced upon slaves and the use of prostitutes. Male and female prostitution and sexual contact between adults and children were relatively ordinary in Roman society at that period.

Under Roman law, divorce was a simple matter, but as Mark contains Jesus's instruction against divorce, (Mark 10:1—12), Christians would have been marrying for life. They would have also been living by the instruction to love one another and lead quiet lives, keeping to themselves and engaging in simple work. ("Work with your hands," Paul suggests.) In other words, they would have been doing everything they could to keep out of the way so that they could practice their faith unmolested.

Unfortunately for them, their groups were concentrated in poorer areas along the Via Aurelia and the Via Appia, which were low and dank. For this reason, they were also spared by the fire. Without warning, imperial soldiers would have descended on them, rounded them up and dragged them off to horrible deaths. It was probably in this persecution that Paul died, some fifteen to twenty years after 1 Thessalonians had been written in Athens.

Mark's portrayal of Jesus as a powerful magician, for that's how his gentile audience would have perceived him based on the gospel, would likely have been intended to offer this beleaguered community some protection by suggesting, however indirectly, that they might also possess some of his power, or could call on him in some way that might help them. And as well, his portrayal as a miracle worker who was not a common magician because he did not charge money would have been intended to identify his works as *theourgia*.

But which of the miracles stories are true? All? None? Any?

Despite the anti-magic laws, magicians were commonplace,

and stories about them circulated constantly, just as stories about healers, mediums and psychics do now. On the rare occasions when a given magician's spells caused a noticeable change of some kind, word would have spread, and we do have records of some famous miracle workers, such as Apollonius of Tyana, who received a *bios* from the philosopher Philostratus that chronicled miracles similar to those of Jesus, and was apparently written to counter his growing influence.

In that era, it was commonplace for magicians to raise the dead, as the story of Apollonius confirms. In his *Life of Apollonius of Tyana*, Philostratus says that he brought the dead back to life and rose from the dead himself—and, in fact, lived a life so much like the life of Jesus that there has long been a question about whether or not the entire story is an invention, in that it was written in the first century, after the Christian stories were already circulating. Nevertheless, the raising of the dead was a common motif, even in the Old Testament where two such acts were attributed to the prophet Elisha. Osiris raised his son Horus from the dead, and the father of medicine, Asclepius, was said to raise the dead. (In fact, as will be seen, the collapse of his cult coincides with the spread of Jesus's in the third century.)

So what was going on? So little was known in those days about death that trickery would have been easy, and anyone in possession of any sharp-smelling substance would have been able to restore people who were unconscious. That the heart circulates blood and causes a pulse was unknown at the time, so anybody who understood the significance of the slight movement in the neck or wrist would have been able to tell if somebody was only unconscious.

Smelling salts are first mentioned by Pliny the Elder in his *Naturalis Historia*, and were probably in use long before then. They would not have been part of general knowledge, but rather kept in the secret troves of magicians and physicians, whose practices were closely related.

A magician or physician, if he had basic diagnostic knowledge, would have been able to determine which "corpses" might be resuscitated by simply checking for a heartbeat or testing for a shallow breath. It must be remembered that it was not until very recently that clear determination of death was possible. Throughout the nineteenth century and before, burials were often belled so that, if the person in the coffin awoke, they could signal for help. When Jesus raises the son of the Widow of Nain, Luke says that he "went up and touched the bier they were carrying him on," then shouted to him to get up. That is to say, he got close enough to determine the boy's true state, and then proceeded to raise him. Did he revive an unconscious person with smelling salts, what Pliny called *Hammoniacus sal*?

The miracles Jesus performed are hardly the only thing about him that is mysterious. Among the other strange things are what happened to him in the gap that appears in his life between the ages of twelve and thirty. After the temple story, he disappears from his own narrative for eighteen years. When he reappears, he is returning from his baptism by John and his forty days in the desert. He is not just a changed man, but a spectacularly revised human being, now possessed of soul-stirring insight, in possession of extraordinary oratorical skills and great spiritual authority, and capable of feats that to this day astonish the world.

The most obvious explanation for this is that the Jesus described in the gospels is a *bios* exaggerated from the life story of a beloved rabbi who was unjustly executed by the Romans. If so, this would not have been done simply out of respect, but to counter the growing threat the cult of Roman imperial divinity posed to Jewish religious purity. Under this scenario, the Jesus of the gospels is a fictional character built on the life of a real person who was already much revered in the Jewish community, a revolutionary and a man of God.

However, this doesn't explain the transcendence of the Beatitudes or the subtle spiritual path hidden in the parables. The gospels must in part be a *bios*, but it seems to me that they are not just the enhanced biography of an ordinary man, but the story a genius who revolutionized human ethics.

The Infancy Gospel, as I have discussed, paints a picture—once the miracles attributed to him are stripped away —of a brilliant, oppressed and angry child. Then, at the age of twelve, he goes to the temple and astonishes the learned men there with the brilliance of his questions. When his parents try to chastise him for walking away from them, he declares his mission. But the mission doesn't start. Instead, the brilliant questioner, the astonisher of the learned, completely disappears for those eighteen mysterious years.

What did he do, then? Sepphoris was being rebuilt by Herod Antipas, and any *tekton* living in Nazareth would likely have walked the few miles to the city to work on construction projects. So was that the life of Jesus then—to work as a laborer? If so, what happened to change him so radically?

If he was in Sepphoris, he would have been working to turn a Jewish city that had been razed to the ground during a rebellion into a Hellenized Roman one. Underpaid, little more than a slave, but with a mind filled with insight, understanding, and knowledge of scripture, he would likely have become even more bitter as a young man than he had been as a child. The injustice and forced impiety that were integral to Jewish life in the Roman state may well have fueled an anger that grew into a passion, finally driving him to revolutionary fervor.

Many observers have noted that brilliant children have a highly developed sense of justice. Kazimierz Dabrowski, in *Personality-Shaping Through Positive Disintegration*, makes the point that highly intelligent individuals feel oppressed in societies organized around power and achievement—the very sort of environment in which Jesus lived.

The temple infancy story tells us that at the age of twelve he already had his mission worked out in his mind, and was more committed to it than he was to his own family. When his parents found him in the temple after three days of desperate searching and chastised him for not telling them where he was going, it didn't even occur to him to apologize.

Given his level of intelligence and insight, he may have thought—probably correctly—that a child would not be able to fulfill the goal that he had set himself, to lift the Roman curse that had fallen on his people. The fact that he couldn't succeed even if he raised an army would have been driven home by his knowledge of what had happened to Sepphoris when he was a child. Therefore, it would seem likely that Celsus's claim that he went to Egypt, supporting himself by hiring out as a worker so that he could learn magic, is accurate. From twelve until sometime in his twenties, it's conceivable that he worked in Galilee, probably with his father and brothers. Then, perhaps because he'd had enough of the oppression, he set out to empower himself. The only real option open would have been to become a magician powerful enough to draw followers and use them as the core of what he might have hoped would become a general uprising. When he returned, he increased his power by going to the Jordan, the holy river of the Jews, and having himself washed in it by the famous and powerful seer John the Baptist. In those days, such a baptism was much more than a symbolic ritual. When John bathed him in those waters, he also bathed him in the truth. He would have felt that cleansing deeply, and seen it as empowering him to do the work of God. During his time in the desert, meant to mirror the time the Jews wandered in the Sinai, he would have worked out his plan of action.

He would have been under no illusions about the odds

against him, which is likely why his fervor was so great, and why his family and friends thought, when he returned to Nazareth, that he had gone insane—that is, had been infested by a demon—and proposed to confine him.

If this is at least a reasonable approximation of what happened, what Jesus had now become was a brilliant revolutionary, equipped with magical skills and inflamed by his baptism. From the gospel accounts, he gathered his first followers to him simply by the force of his will, then went on to excite great multitudes with his oratory, and the performance of acts of magic that stunned the entire region. But, as we have seen, he had to be careful that stories of his magic not reach the ears of the authorities—which, incidentally, accounts for what William Wrede first identified as "the messianic secret" in his 1901 book of the same name. Wrede believed that his continually asking those upon whom he performed healings to tell nobody was to conceal his identity as the messiah. Far more likely it was as it appears, which was to conceal his identity as a magician.

He would also have already seen that John's spreading fame was what had caused him to be imprisoned and killed, which would have been another reason for him to be secretive. He planned to build his revolution underground, away from the prying eyes of the Romans and their Jewish upper-class supporters.

The cue for him to go into action on his own appears to have been the arrest of John. In Mark 1, the moment that John is arrested, Jesus begins walking along the shore of the Sea of Galilee gathering followers, then goes to Capernaum, a small community on its shore, enters the assembly-house and on the Sabbath stands up and starts teaching.

We do not know the first words of his ministry, but Mark reports that they caused amazement due to the fact that he was not teaching through the medium of scriptural reference, as was the normal practice, but rather on his own authority—an approach entirely consistent with what he had told his parents in the temple, that he was "about my father's business."

The first miracle then took place, probably when somebody took violent exception to his approach and began screaming at him. Jesus shouted him down with such force and eloquence that he ceased to oppose him. (Mark 1:24—26)

The gospel author has a demon cry out from within the man, "What do you want with us, Jesus of Nazareth, have you come to destroy us?" Then is added the phrase, "I know who you are—the Holy One of God" (Mark 1:24). But perhaps that last is a later addition, because if Jesus was preaching what is later recorded in more detail, he was talking sedition—and this in Galilee where the danger of opposing the Romans would have been fresh in the minds of his listeners, so this miracle is probably not like the relief of the insane that would take place so often over the next few years, but rather the successful conversion, through the force of his oratory and the eloquence of his argument, of somebody who feared the Romans.

Immediately thereafter, he leaves the synagogue and goes to the house of Andrew and Simon, where Andrew's mother was sick with what is described as "a fever." There is no way to tell exactly what was wrong, but when Jesus takes her hand, she's cured and returns to her household chores. (Mark 1:30—31)

It's not hard to picture the scene: she's miserable and burning with fever when her sons and their newfound friend burst in talking excitedly about what just transpired in the assembly house—a man shouting Jesus down, rid of a demon before their eyes by their new master, a truly great magician. She sees Jesus, possibly for the first time. He is still full of excitement at his first victory—and he sees her suffering, and as would be the case for the rest of his life, immediately tries to help her. He touches her and tells her she's healed—and it works. She gets up from her bed, the fever gone. The placebo effect has worked, at least for a time. As she is never mentioned again, we have no way of knowing if she was permanently cured or not.

Word about this event spreads fast, and in the next verse, Jesus is being mobbed by the infirm and the afflicted, all clamoring for cures. His oratory has worked, his message has inspired, and his magic has been effective. In other words, his ministry has begun.

He has thus gone from being an illegitimate child uneasily accepted into his family to an inspired messianic leader. In some way, he has been truly inspired, but not to take his message to the upper reaches of society. On the contrary, he speaks often of his disdain for them and his love of the common people. He generally teaches from his own mind rather than from scripture, which is why when he was in the synagogue in Capernaum it was said that "he taught with authority, not as teachers of the law," (Mark 1:22), and when he returned to Nazareth, his family and friends asked, "Where did this man get these things?" (Mark 6:2)

His second great miracle, and the first overtly physical one, is recorded in the first verses of Mark 2. With the crowd swelling and surging around him, he has retreated to a house where he is presumably enacting unrecorded miracles. A man is brought, lying on a pallet. To get him close to Jesus, his friends remove part of the roof of the house and lower him down into Jesus's presence.

He is described as *paralytikos* in the text, unable to move. I include this miracle for a specific reason, which is that it describes both a physical cure and a forgiveness of sin. The sequence of events in Mark 2 is as follows: The man is brought before Jesus lying helpless. Jesus reacts to the faith of his friends by saying, "Son, your sins are forgiven." He then perceives that some "teachers of the law" are thinking that he has blasphemed, because only God can forgive sins. It is portrayed as an act of magical mind reading in the gospel, but it wouldn't have taken a man of Jesus's intelligence to surmise what the scholars were thinking. He then says, "Which is easier: to say to this paralyzed man, 'Your sins are forgiven,' or to say, 'Get up, take your mat and walk?'" (Mark 2: 9) Jesus is teaching here that these two seemingly unrelated acts are actually the same thing. So was the young man in a state of hysteria, but not physically paralyzed? This is certainly possible, because the forgiveness of his sins does free him from his paralysis. Or is the paralysis symbolic of a guilty inability to face some dreadful thing he has done and ask forgiveness for it?

In Jesus's time and in his teaching, physical illness, psychological dysfunction, and spiritual duress were not seen as separate from one another, and it is only by understanding this that we can gain perspective on the meaning of the miracles. Thus there is no reason to assume that the young man was *not* cured of an actual paralysis by being granted forgiveness for his sins by an authority that he felt he could trust, namely Jesus.

Another such miracle appears in Matthew 8:2: "A man with leprosy came and knelt before him and said, '"Lord, if you are willing, you can make me clean."'"

The man is described as *lepros* in the text—that is, suffering from one of dozens of skin disease that in those days were lumped under the general term "leprosy."

Virtually everyone in the Roman Empire experienced one kind of chronic stress or another, and in Galilee at that time, with ruthless taxation, enforced religious apostasy, chronic malnutrition and hunger added to the terror of brutal Roman enforcement techniques, stress levels would have been extreme. Among Jesus's audiences would have been people who had been forced into crippling debt and lived in fear that the land bequeathed to them by their fathers would soon fall into the hands of the Roman and Jewish elite; others who had sold their children and wives into slavery to meet their debts; many who had at one time or another experienced the harsh crowd control methods of the Romans; and many who feared that their misfortunes were being visited upon them by Jehovah because they had engaged in compulsory worship of the emperor. Add to this the fact that they were almost all parasitized, and thus suffering from reduced stamina in a world that required constant heavy physical work, and were afraid of a myriad of gods and demons, and living in squalid circumstances, and they would have certainly been willing to believe in a wonder worker like Jesus, with his conviction, compelling delivery, and magical skills.

Chronic stress leads to high cortisol levels, which in turn can cause rashes. Sounds innocuous enough, but in a world without hygiene, scratching with dirty fingernails, rubbing irritated skin against soiled cloth, and the action of vermin such as flies, lice, and fleas all had the potential to transform a simple case of hives into to any number of serious skin disorders.

When Jesus cures the man, it would seem that the disease, which was probably a case of hives that had become badly infected, spontaneously retreats. Had it actually been Hansen's Disease, it's hard to believe that even the most dramatic and convincing healer could have changed anything. As there has been a case of Hansen's identified in a burial of around 50 A.D. outside the walls of Jerusalem, we know that the illness existed in that place and time. How widespread it was, there is no way to tell. What the leper in this story suffered from is also impossible to know, but whatever it was, if the tale the gospel writers heard and recorded has any truth in it, the affliction must have been responsive to the placebo effect.

Jesus is careful to tell the man to keep his story to himself, but he goes out and immediately does the natural thing: he proclaims his cure to everyone. He does this, because, in that period, "lepers" were untouchable and kept out of the normal social flow. The only work allowed to them was begging. So his sudden and completely unexpected release from such a tragic situation would have been something he would want to announce to the world.

Jesus, however, had engaged in a magical act, in contravention of both Jewish and Roman law, and naturally did not want word of such an action to spread too widely.

Given the way skin disease and stress are related, this is another miracle that may have actually happened in the physical world, and therefore the way Mark describes the even greater increase in Jesus's popularity that followed might be quite true to life. Additionally, the more cures Jesus accomplished, the more people would have been convinced of his powers, and the more effective he would have become.

It must be noted that Jesus does not say to the leper, as he did to the paralyzed man, "Your sins are forgiven." (Mark 2:5). This is because, like the other miracles I have chosen, the miracle of the leper is closer to being purely a chronicle of an actual, physical event rather than also referring also to spiritual change, as does the miracle of the paralyzed man in Mark 2. Only in verse 11, he finally says to the man "I tell you, get up, take your mat and go home," but the first point he makes is that the man's sin is forgiven.

The next miracle I wish to discuss appears in Matthew, Luke and John, and is included in Q. This is the healing at a distance of the Centurion's *paidon*, a Greek word that is used in Matthew and Luke but not in John, which in common usage at the time meant a boy lover. A commonplace practice among the Romans when they were writing, by John's time it was more of a marginal behavior, and frowned upon by many. In John, the word is changed to *huios*, son, presumably to conceal the sexual implications lest it appear that Jesus found such behavior acceptable. The sexual austerity counseled by the

Didache, which appeared at about the same time, certainly did not approve of it.

It has been generally assumed that the hypothetical Q gospel contains the earliest Jesus material, but I doubt that this story is an early one. If it was, it would surely have appeared in Mark, in particular because his *bios* of Jesus was intended for gentiles and therefore Romans, as the Markian author most probably wrote in Rome. Had the story of a centurion appealing to Jesus and getting help been current then, Mark certainly would have used it. He seems to have been writing, at least to some extent, to educate gentiles about his sect. This would be why he is at such pains to put the kindness of Jesus on display, and to show that his activities were not offensive to the Roman state. If he had been able to show that Jesus had been kind to a Roman, he surely would have done so.

By the time Matthew and Luke were being written, Jerusalem had fallen and the Jews been driven out of Judea. If the Jesus sect was to survive, it had more than ever to appeal to the broader population. Thus the story of how Jesus, in his kindness, offered healing to someone beloved of a Roman centurion appears in the narrative.

This miracle would have been a healing at a distance. In 2005, Duke University Health published the results of a study that in part included healing at a distance. The study, updated in 2016, concluded that "distant prayer and the bedside use of music, imagery and touch (MIT therapy) did not have a significant effect upon the primary clinical outcome observed in patients undergoing certain heart procedures..." Of the subject patients, 182 received off-site intercessory prayer only. While those receiving healing touch had better long-term outcomes than those who did not, prayer appeared to have no effect.

Of course, an initial study like this, with a relatively small study group (a total of under a thousand patients) is not conclusive, but it is suggestive that healing modalities like prayer are unlikely to have a dramatic effect on disease.

The literature of healing at a distance is enormous. I know distance healers myself, and some of their subjects have told me personally that the method is effective. When you strip away any possibility of a placebo effect, though, you get results like the Duke study.

Combined with the fact that the story has a clear political motive, as neither the power of suggestion nor the placebo effect apply in a case of distant healing, and modern studies show that traditional methods like prayer do not appear to be effective, it seems most likely that this event never took place. It probably shouldn't be part of Q either, as it is unlikely that it was added to Matthew and Luke from a very early source, but was rather original to Matthew and included in Luke from that source, then amended again to remove suggestion of the centurion's pederasty for inclusion in John, in the same way that the birth story was changed from Mark's "son of Mary" to "son of Joseph" in the later gospels.

Nevertheless, as a person who has witnessed many things that aren't supposed to happen, I cannot say that I think that the miracle was impossible. There are many healing miracles recorded in the Catholic tradition in which I was raised.

This miracle, also, continues the great theme of faith that runs through the entirety of the teaching. "Truly, I tell you, I have not found anyone in Israel with such great faith." (Matt. 8:10)

I might note that the Greek word *pistis*, used here, appears throughout the gospels, and is used to describe not a state of belief, but one of persuasion. The *Theological Dictionary of the New Testament* identifies it with reliability, and the way it is used suggests that when Jesus praised somebody for their faith, he was saying that they had shown that they believed that his claims about himself as possessing the power of God could be relied upon. It is very different from the word *doxasia*, or belief, which means something closer to adherence to a structural orthodoxy. The word *doxasia* is not used in the gospels. When Jesus says, for example, "If you believe, you will receive whatever you ask for in prayer," (Matt. 21:22) he uses *pisteuonton*, which refers to having faith, and this usage is consistent across the gospels. So the success of the miracles is not dependent on adherence to a rigid set of beliefs, but rather on the much deeper identification of *pistis*, or confidence in Jesus.

In addition to the healing miracles, there are numerous nature miracles in the gospels, including the multiplication of food, the stilling of the storm and the walking on water. It is to this latter story that I will now turn.

"Shortly before dawn, Jesus went out to them, walking on the lake. When the disciples saw him walking on the lake, they were terrified. 'It's a ghost,' they said, and cried out in fear." (Matt. 14: 25—26)

Surely this must be a fabrication. But is it? Given that we now possess a long history of levitations, it's not clear that such a thing is as impossible as it seems. Of course, along with the stories of levitation purported to be true, there is a fascinating trove of fraud.

As levitation is considered a *siddhi*, or accomplishment, in Yoga, claims of this ability must go back a very long time, although no convincing examples of the *siddhi* have been recorded in modern times, say, on film or videotape. Yogi Subbayah Pullavar was observed to levitate before a crowd in June of 1936, but it turned out to be a magic trick involving the use of a concealed iron bar. Yogananda, in his *Autobiography of a Yogi* recounts a number of stories of levitation, but, like the Jesus story, they are verified only by observation of a few witnesses. There is a story of Buddha levitating to cross a river, but again, no record of witnesses.

This, however, is not true of all levitation stories, and some have been extensively witnessed. Three of these are Saint Theresa of Avila, Saint Francis of Assisi and Saint Joseph of Cupertino. There are also the stories of Padre Pio, now Saint Padre Pio. All four were also stigmatics, that is to say, at one time or another in their lives, they developed signs of Jesus's wounds on their bodies.

All of them would have believed every word of the gospels implicitly, and the stigmata indicated that all were religious ecstatics. Jesus, also, lived in an ecstatic religious state. He believed, as Matthew records, that he was the literally an aspect of God. When he called himself "son of man" in Matthew he is referring to the one use of this phrase in the Bible, in Daniel 7, "In my vision at night I looked, and there before me was one like a son of man, coming with the clouds of heaven. He approached the Ancient of Days and was led into his presence." (Dan. 7:13—14) In other words, he thought himself not to be human, but rather an aspect of God that appeared to be human —at least, that's what the gospel author wants to communicate. The specific phrase "son of man" is used 81 times in the canonical gospels, so it would seem inevitable that it actually was how he described himself, and what he believed himself to be. A belief like that, that he actually *was* God, would take religious ecstasy to a very high level indeed. Later, his conviction would be so strong that it would lead him to his death, and the despairing cry toward the end to God his father, quoting Psalm 22, "My God, my God, why have you forsaken me?"

As so much of his magic worked, and things like his levitation might have actually happened, his belief in himself as being exactly what he said he was would, by the end of his life, have been implicit. It would be why he would be willing to risk going to Jerusalem in the first place, which I will discuss in detail in a later chapter.

Could religious ecstasy, then, lead to an ability to distort reality so extreme that it enables levitation? This would imply that the body, which is basically a big bag of water organized around a frame of bones (all of this quite heavy, or course) would have to entirely change its nature, losing all that weight.

But how? How could all those heavy molecules suddenly shed their mass?

Personally, I don't see how it could happen, but the many witnesses to the saintly levitations suggest that it can.

Saint Joseph of Cupertino was a seventeenth century Franciscan Friar and mystic. He was a religious ecstatic so intense that he was dismissed from the Capuchins, apparently because his continual ecstasies were unendurably disruptive to the peace of the order. His levitations were extensively witnessed, to the point that he came to the attention of the Inquisition, as magical flight was believed to be a result of witchcraft.

Saint Alphonsus of Ligouri levitated while saying mass before an entire congregation, so it's hard to think that this simply didn't happen.

In his book *Padre Pio and America*, Frank Reggio reports that numerous allied pilots saw a friar flying above the town of San Giovanni Rotondo, and would turn back in face of the apparition. As there was believed to be a German ammunition dump near the town, the commanding general of the United Air Command, Bernardo Rosini, eventually flew a mission himself and observed the levitating friar. After the war, he became a devotee of Padre Pio.

At least, so the story goes. There was no "United Air Command" in the Allied Air Forces during World War II. While there was an organization called the Italian Co-Belligerent Air Force, formed by officers loyal to the royalist Badoglio government in 1943, it never flew combat missions, and did not fly any missions over Italy at all.

So the question of whether or not the flying friar flew must remain up in the air, and along with it, the other levitation stories. And yet...I cannot quite dismiss them as hoaxes or, in the case of Jesus, a fiction created or heard by Mark to further the claim of divinity, and then repeated by all the other gospel writers.

Some of the miracles happened. Certainly, some of the exorcisms, and probably some of the hands-on healings. As a religious ecstatic, absolutely convinced of his origin and his role in the world, Jesus brought intense conviction to his ministry. That, combined with his eloquence, intelligence, and a message that was bound to stir the hearts of the oppressed, made him a formidable presence indeed in the powerless and desperate little worlds of Galilee and Judea.

He offered hope. He offered teaching that was capable of completely revising a person's self-image. He offered, to those short-lived, universally diseased and terribly vulnerable people, the promise of some deliverance from their suffering.

Of course he accomplished miracles, and some of his healings must have been entirely real. But the greatest of them was his life itself, and the astonishing, near-impossible fact that the story of this one messianic claimant—one of many who lived, preached and were executed in Palestine in those troubled times—not only entered oral and then written memory, but was then amplified into a religion that has changed human life and human history as very profoundly as it has.

Did this happen because he was indeed something more than a brilliant human being? What was Jesus, that he could inspire such faith that infections could be cured and paralytics made to walk—even if the infections started with psychosomatic illnesses and the paralysis was hysterical?

The miracles were meant to establish Jesus's credibility as someone with special powers. But they don't offer anything deeper to the seeker after inner truth. That task is reserved to the remarkable and powerful stories known as the parables. They are remarkable because they can open an inner door in us that is usually closed, and enable us to actually see the interior path toward the realm of heaven. Once we see it, we can follow it. (This is called the kingdom of heaven in most gospel translations, but I will, for the most part, call it a "realm")

Jesus offers a realm of heaven that is within us right now. His great good news is that, no matter how hard outer life may be, we can live from a peace that is within us, and is eternal.

Let's explore.

6

THE KEYS TO THE KINGDOM

The parables are living spiritual organisms that can enter a person and work deep soul changes. The miracles relieved the suffering of the body, which is disease. The parables relieve the suffering of the soul, which is aimlessness. Through them we can find a clear inner response to that most ancient of challenges: "Know thyself." These two words were inscribed on the Temple of Apollo at Delphi, and it is this essential quest that is also at the core of the spiritual journey of the parables.

I will discuss the four parables that most clearly reveal the inner path of the Jesus teaching. They are: the sower, the weeds, the mustard seed, and the laborers in the vineyard.

The Parable of the Sower reads in Mark as follows:

"A farmer went out to sow his seed. As he was scattering the seed, some fell along the path, and the birds came and ate it up. Some fell on rocky places, where it did not have much soil. It sprang up quickly, because the soil was shallow. But when the sun came up, the plants were scorched, and they withered because they had no root. Other seed fell among thorns, which grew up and choked the plants, so that they did not bear grain.

Still other seed fell on good soil. It came up, grew and produced a crop, some multiplying thirty, some sixty, some a hundred times." (Mark 4:1—20)

Jesus then explains to his students that "to those on the outside, everything is said in parables." He then quotes 12 Isaiah 6:9—10 which says that outsiders may hear and see but not understand, because if they did, they might turn—that is to say, recognize the truth and be forgiven.

Two verses later, Jesus reassures his disciples that "the secret of the Kingdom of God has been given to you," (Mark 4:11). He proceeds to explain the parable to them: "Don't you understand this parable? How then will you understand any parable? The farmer sows the word. Some people are like seed along the path, where the word is sown. As soon as they hear it, Satan comes and takes away the word that was sown in them. Others, like seed sown on rocky places, hear the word and at once receive it with joy. But since they have no root, they last only a short time."

He goes on to explain that "others' hear the word, but "like seed sown among thorns." That is to say, the worries of this life, the deceitfulness of wealth and the desires for things coveted choke it off in them. They do not give up their angers and desires and follow the new ethics of the realm that he laid out in the Beatitudes with which he began his ministry.

Then comes Mark 4:20: "Others, like seed sown on good soil, hear the word, accept it, and produce a crop..."

But why does Jesus first tell his students that they are among the elect, then that there is some danger, presumably to the truth itself, if non-elect are allowed to know it—then say that *they* don't know it, and then proceed to reveal it to them?

The contradiction in the passage can only be resolved if one assumes that Jesus sees the "apostles" and the "outsiders" as different parts of the same person. The apostle is the interior individual who has embraced the teaching and understands it.

The outsiders are the various layers of personality that live in the ordinary world.

The seed that is sown on the roadside and immediately lost is the part of us that is directed exclusively toward the material world. As soon as this level of mind hears something that suggests that it must look beyond the material wealth it has worked so hard to acquire, it is like that rich young man whom Jesus advised to give his possessions to the poor in order to gain treasure in heaven. "When the young man heard this, he went away sad, because he had great wealth." (Matt. 19:21—22)

The birds that eat these seeds, because they are in flight, represent whatever draws us away from our aim, which, in the world of the parables, is always the same: to discover ourselves. Later in the story, they will be called Satan, because that is who draws us away from the great quest to know oneself and thus be free.

The next group of seeds fall on rocky soil and spring up immediately, but as they have no anchor, they soon wither away. Rocky soil is the unwillingness to begin one's journey toward the realm of peace within.

But why do we turn away from it? Everybody wants peace... don't they?

The "good soil" of the parable is the insight necessary to understand why we so often don't want inner peace at all. Who in us doesn't want peace?

When we look at it, we actually don't know. Why *don't* we want to live in peace? But it's true. We don't. This again brings in that ancient piece of advice: "Know thyself." This is the "good soil," but where does it come from? The parable tells us. We must start with the most basic truth about us, which is that we are born of the Earth—that's why it's called "good soil."

The parables, seemingly so obscure, are actually practical teaching tools. For example, if one looks inside oneself, one can find all of the different "seeds" that fall here and there. A part of me does not want to embrace the ethics of the Beatitudes. I don't want to think about the poor, it makes it harder for me to enjoy the pleasures of my life. The person who is out in the cold can stay there because, after all, I've worked hard to earn my money and I can do what I want with it. This is my ego telling me that I am more than my fellow man, and tempting me to harden my heart so that I will not experience compassion and have to face the needs of the other person.

I recall a saying of my wife's: "Each of us is all we have." Embrace that, and everybody's life becomes as important to you as your own. You can't do it, though, unless you can also accept that the world is filled with a torrent of need that you can never hope to fill.

Although I cannot stop the burning of the forests or the souring of the oceans, or bring cool air to the arctic or rain to parched farms, or much improve the constricted lives of so many billions of us, I can *want* these things, and when I do, I am moving toward my place in the realm of heaven, for I am walking the path laid down by this parable.

Once one understands how to use parables, which is by seeing them *internally,* their role as the hidden path to "the realm that is within you" is made plain.

In the second parable we're exploring, the Parable of the Weeds, Jesus says, "The realm of heaven is like a man who sowed good seed in his field. But while everyone was sleeping, his enemy came and sowed weeds among the wheat, and went away. When the wheat sprouted and formed heads, the weeds also appeared."

The farmer realizes that an enemy has sabotaged his crop. But he tells his servants not to pull up the weeds lest they also uproot the wheat. "Let both grow together until the harvest. At that time I will tell the harvesters: 'First collect the weeds and tie them in bundles to be burned; then gather the wheat and bring it into my barn.'" (Matt. 13: 24—30)

In this parable, the field is the experience of life, the sower is the person living the life, the weeds are distractions of all kinds, sown by his enemy, which is any part of him that does not strengthen his soul.

The servants are the parts of him who have his best interests at heart—that is to say, his inner quest to find the realm of heaven. When they ask him if they should gather in the weeds, he tells them to let them grow. He says this because we cannot ignore the things about ourselves that impede our journey, but rather need to see them clearly enough that we can draw them right out of us. If we do that before we truly understand ourselves, we'll destroy the wheat, too, which is the wisdom that also grows within us.

Perhaps the most famous of all the parables is the Mustard Seed. Also a wonderful thing to understand, because when it is living inside you, in your knowledge, it is truly a "wonderful counselor," as is said of the messiah in Isaiah 9.

"What is the realm of God like? What shall I compare it to? It is like a mustard seed, which a man took and planted in his garden. It grew and became a tree, and the birds perched in its branches." (Luke 13: 18—19)

But the mustard plant grows into a small bush. It doesn't become a tree now and it didn't then, so what is really meant here? First, it is a sign that there is a secret to be discovered—something that, until recent centuries, anybody reading the passage would at least have been able to suspect. Now, though, in our urban world, with most of us living far distant from anywhere that mustard might be growing, we simply accept the idea that a mustard plant can become a tree.

Recall in the Parable of the Sower, the birds flew about everywhere, dropping the seeds of inner knowledge and scattering them, which is why they were also identified with Satan. These birds of desire and regret have a deep life in the Bible: "We have escaped like a bird from the fowler's snare; the snare has been broken, and we have escaped." (Psalm 124:7) Then, in Revelation, "I saw an angel standing in the sun, who cried in a loud voice to all the birds flying in the air, 'Come, gather together for the great supper of God.'" (Rev. 19—17)

In the Mustard Seed, the birds of desire gather into the shelter of "the tree," that is to say, the shelter of the soul. Self knowledge means that we accept ourselves. The birds are the things about ourselves that we'd prefer to let fly away. Knowing oneself is accepting oneself, including the parts that we don't like. If you long to take what another has, for example, you certainly don't have to do it, but on the Jesus path, you do have to accept that you want to.

The parable contains a hidden miracle: a mustard plant turning into a huge tree. The meaning here, it seems to me, is that the seed sown on the fertile ground of a seeker after self-knowledge will grow as knowledge grows, no matter how small it is to start.

Hidden in this parable, with its image of a great tree full of the settled birds of desire, is a promise of peace. To accept the things about ourselves that we don't like is to touch the peace of heaven. But only to touch it. There is a deeper promise.

My wife, who was a scholar of the gospels, considered joy to be the core message of the Jesus teaching. If she was asked the difference between happiness and joy, she would say, "Happiness is getting that new TV you've been longing for. Joy is holding a baby. That's the difference." And therein lies, also, the hidden promise of the birds at rest in the tree.

What might bring them to rest? However can we accept ourselves so completely as this?

When Jesus says, "Let the little children come to me, and do not hinder them, for the realm of God belongs to such as these," he is speaking to the innocence within us all, that lies behind all the cares of our lives, and which we can still see so clearly when we hold a baby. The joy you experience when a little one smiles back at you is the same joy you will find in the heaven that lies within you. A baby is too innocent not to be happy. The keys to the realm can be found in the smile of one of those little ones. Life has closed the door to our innocence.

"Consider the lilies of the field, how they grow. They do not labor or spin. Yet I tell you, not even Solomon in all his splendor was dressed like one of these." (Matt. 6:28—29). We think, how can we be like that? We need to work or we'll die. We need a house. We can't live in some field.

This is true of the outer self, but not the inner. The inner self belongs to the field of life in the same way that the lily does to the flower-field. It is finding what is really in that field—the love in us that he calls "the lilies"—that the verse expresses so powerfully and poetically.

When I think of Jesus in his struggle, I always return to how it must have felt within him to be able to utter words that reflect such profound surrender. The more he taught, the greater his danger became, but he lived as a lily, innocently bowing to the wind that was blowing ever harder in his life.

The deepest message of the story of the lilies is that we don't need to *act*, we need to *accept*. So this extraordinary passage is also intended to free us from the illusion that God provides and God punishes. The clouds fly across the sky, the sun and the moon go in their courses, changes come and go. "Man comes and tills the fields and lies beneath. And after many a summer dies the swan." So says the poet Tennyson in his "Tithonus." Surrendering to our place in nature is an act of love. It is the greatest act of the heart. And that is what the passage means. As the lilies bow in the field, the birds of desire come to rest, accepting their limits, in the tree of the soul.

Jesus's teaching is an attempt to free us from the prison of the idea that we are somehow at fault for existing, a task at which he both succeeded and failed. Succeeded, because anyone "who has ears to hear" can follow the path of the parables. Failed, because he did not succeed in defeating the ancient belief that we fell irrevocably from the innocence of "the lilies" when we found self-awareness.

The good news of his teaching, summed up, is that we *can regain the innocence of Eden*—not in the outer world, but by returning to the peace that is at the center of every heart.

And how do we do that? "Know thyself."

As will be seen, the ancient world did not grasp the opportunity Jesus was offering. On the contrary, as the Jesus teaching became Christianity, rather than lessening the tyrannies of the Roman Empire, it joined itself to them. Why this happened and why it continued for so long will be the subject of a later chapter.

On a personal level, the value of the Jesus teaching remains today just as it was when it appeared. To understand it, though, requires a new way of reading the stories and parables.

The most useful parable in this regard is the Workers in the Vineyard.

This complex and subtle teaching begins at Matthew 19, verse 28, when Jesus assures his students that when the Son of Man is sitting on his "glorious throne," the twelve who have "followed me" will also sit on thrones and judge others. He adds that everyone who has left home and family to follow him will inherit eternal life. The next sentence, though, contains a warning: "But many who are first will be last, and many who are last will be first." (Matt. 19:30)

He goes on to explain this by giving voice to the body of the parable: "For the realm of heaven is like a landowner who went out early in the morning to hire workers for his vineyard. He agreed to pay them a penny for the day and sent them into his vineyard." Matt. 19:20) Then later in the morning, he hired more workers, then again at noon and at three in the afternoon, then yet again at five. "When evening came, the owner of the vineyard said to his foreman, 'Call the workers and pay them their wages, beginning with the last ones hired and going on to the first.' (Matt. 20:8)

When all the workers, from the ones who had worked only an hour or so to the ones who had been working all day each received the same sum, the ones who had been at it since morning were understandably disgruntled. The owner responds that they agreed on a penny, and says that he has the right to be generous if he wishes. "So the last will be first, and the first will be last."

These words refer, in the language of the parables, to an overturning of our inner order. As to what it would mean to do that, the story is very clear: in one moment, Jesus promises the apostles that they will be enthroned and sit in judgment of others. In the next, he explains that the judges will become the judged.

The parable itself is an explanation of what this means and what it is for. When the owner of the vineyard explains himself, saying "I am good," he is saying that he is satisfied with his understanding of who he is. He will not judge himself. He has no need. He has accepted himself and therefore will give his understanding equally to every aspect of himself.

This is why he can call himself "good." It is because he knows every aspect of himself and values all.

The generosity of the owner of the vineyard is to give his inner workmen—the parts of him that are enacting his life journey—an equal chance to discover what they need to discover, and therefore an equal reward when they do.

Once we understand what we need in the spirit, we're on our way to finding a real life aim, and with it true purpose and direction in the quest to know oneself.

But how is this quest to be undertaken? Where does the Jesus path within us start?

The next stop on the Jesus path is really two stops that are profoundly—although probably not intentionally—linked.

The Gospel of Mary has been pieced together out of a series of finds of various kinds, and remains fragmentary. The Gospel of Thomas, buried very much like a Djinn in a bottle for two thousand years in a jar in Egypt, is complete.

Mary's gospel is among the deepest expressions of the heart's search for peace that has ever been written. Thomas is among the ancient world's greatest acts of the mind.

7

THE HIDDEN BRIDE

B efore we turn to the Gospel of Mary itself, I would like to explore one of the most enigmatic passages in the whole gospel literature, which is the story that is known as the Marriage Feast at Cana.

What is strange about it is not what it says, but what it doesn't. It once recorded, I believe, the marriage of Jesus, probably to the Mary of the Gospel of Mary. The fragments of this woman's teaching that appear in her gospel, as we shall see, reflect soaring spiritual genius.

Cana is no longer about that marriage, but it is still hidden in the story.

Normally, it is thought of as a miracle story, but I did not include it in the miracles section because it has nothing to do with the actual transformation of water into wine, which was impossible then and remains impossible to this day. In fact, this symbolic event was carried out in one way or another by most of the prior resurrected gods who preceded Jesus. For example, worshipers of the god Dionysus believed that on the night of January 5, the god would miraculously transform water into wine, in commemoration of having done so on the occasion of his wedding with the goddess Ariadne. This belief was so powerful that it survived well into the Christian era. In the fourth century, the Christian writer Epiphanus declared that he himself drank from a spring dedicated to Dionysus that was flowing with wine instead of water.

Cana would seem to be derived from the earlier mysteries. But since water can't actually be transformed into wine, what is it really about?

The jar in which the water becomes wine is not an actual clay pot, of course. It is a human being—each of us and any of us.

Like the parables, the Marriage Feast at Cana can be understood as a description of an internal, or spiritual, event. In fact, what remains of it has only that meaning. What is important is that water is inert and wine is a living liquid, which grows richer and more complex over time.

The ordinary self is like water: it always remains what it is. It is inert, unchanging. The awakened self is like wine. As wine gains depth and subtlety over time, the awakened self gains understanding, growing richer and more complex. But what does it mean to be awakened? It is a matter of *noticing*, which is why the old master of the feast fails to realize that the water has become wine. This is because nobody tells him and he fails to notice. In other words, the transformation takes place in the secrecy of the water jar—in the mind and body of the individual seeking a new inner life.

But how does it come about? We have only to look at the process of wine making, from the growing of the grapes on. First, the seeds must be planted—that is to say, a person must become aware that life has more to offer. When this realization unfolds, the seeds sprout and the vines of self-exploration began to seek through the inner being, growing and exploring. This is the process of engaging in inner and outer search in life, using the outer wisdom of the mind to discover the inner wisdom of the soul.

The vines are growing, but where are the grapes, where is the wine press? In short, how do we turn water into wine? Jesus offers many ways. In fact, the whole of the ethics he presents is devoted to this process—which takes us right back to the Beatitudes.

The eight sayings appear at the beginning of the Gospel of Matthew, in his rendering of the Sermon on the Mount. They are called "beatitudes" from the Latin *beatitude*, a word invented by the Roman orator Marcus Tullius Cicero to designate a blessing. In this book, I do not use the word "blessed" in my rendering of the Beatitudes, but rather "beloved." I do this because in the original gospels the word is not present. It was added in the Latin Vulgate in the sixteenth century, and I think that "beloved" better expresses the feeling of closeness to the love of God that they seem to me to be meant to convey.

Let's look at them a bit more deeply, for a number of them are just the sort of tools we need to engage in the inner process of turning the water of life into the wine of the soul.

The first Beatitude is "Beloved are the spiritual beggars, for they will be welcome in heaven." Externally, in the world Jesus lived in, hunger, as I have pointed out, was almost universal and beggars were everywhere. The theme of the needs of the hungry, both physical and spiritual, is of central importance to his teaching, and to me the word "beggars" conveys more coherently the meaning of the Greek *ptochos* which is used in the gospel. In the time of Jesus, it would have most commonly meant "a beggar."

Internally, the need to know oneself is the mustard seed of the parable. It is the unseen wine press of the Cana story, and why it is called a "feast." It is at Cana that those hungry for inner growth are satisfied.

"Beloved are the sad, for they will be made cheerful." This

is the key to that transformation: you cannot know yourself unless you can find enough inner strength to laugh at your own shortcomings instead of regretting them. My wife, who understood this in her deep heart, always quoted the great fourteenth century

Catholic teacher Meister Eckhart's wonderful sentence, "God laughs and plays," and with good reason. When you can laugh at yourself as a child laughs, you can open your heart to the parts of yourself that you normally will not face, which puts you on the Jesus path.

Most translations of the third Beatitude render the Greek word *praeis* as "meek," leading to the impression that a passive state is required. The Greek word is much more nuanced. Instead of "the meek shall inherit the Earth," a more accurate translation might be "those who are gentle and strong shall inherit the Earth." In the inner language of the gospels, "earth" means that which is passive—that is to say, the same thing as "water" in Cana. It is you are as you are, living as if all there is of you is what is attached to the name your parents gave you. But this is not the whole of you, and only if you are gentle but firm with yourself will all of your goodness and all of your evil come into light—that is, the water will be turned into wine. So these three Beatitudes summarize the secret of transformation.

As the Cana story continues, "Jesus's mother said to him, 'They have no more wine.'"

"Woman, why do you involve me?" Jesus replied. "My hour has not yet come." This is the refusal of the call, a fundamental event in any spiritual journey. It is fear, in this case well justified, for it is the beginning of the journey to his final end—his terrible passion.

His mother knows him with a mother's insight and therefore trusts him completely. She knows that he understands himself, and that he will overcome his fear. Thus, she simply ignores his refusal and tells the servants to do whatever he says.

The transformation of the water, the passive inner life, into the wine of an active journey toward awakening then commences.

The Dionysus story contains nothing like this. So unless there is something similar in the lost mysteries, the Marriage Feast at Cana—that brief story—is probably the most potent description of activating one's inner search in all of ancient literature. Certainly, among the stories that we know it is that.

Now let's turn to what's missing in the story, and therefore to a more literal level. Galilee had very specific wedding customs. After a negotiation between the families, the bride and groom would drink wine from the same cup, which would create their betrothal. The groom would then leave and build a house for himself and his bride, usually adding it to the complex already built by his family over generations. He would then go to the bride and get her and her bridesmaids, and bring them to the new house. The groomsmen would wait at the door while the marriage was consummated. Then a seven-day feast would commence.

It is such a feast that is being described in the Marriage Feast at Cana. But there are some missing elements. Who is the bride? Why is the groom not named?

Could it be that Jesus was the groom, which is why the steward comes to him to discuss the issue with the wine? And what of the wife?

Except in Mark, all three women at the foot of the cross are called Mary: Mary the Mother, Mary Magdalene and Mary the sister of his mother. This number is unlikely to be an accident. Like the Holy Trinity, the three at the foot of the cross reflect the ancient—and very modern—idea of the triad. In the polytheistic religions, the great goddess was triune—that is, she had three natures: Demeter, the goddess of the harvest; Persephone, the goddess of the underworld; and Hecate, the goddess of magic.

Mary the mother would have been the goddess of the

harvest, the fertile one. Mary her sister would have been the goddess of the underworld, the opposite of her sister's sacred fertility. Mary of Magdala, as the wife, would have been the goddess of magic, as it would have been in consort with her that Jesus reached ecstatic union.

Saying 22 of the Thomas gospel sums up the marriage relationship: "When you make the two into one, and when you make the inner as the outer, and the upper as the lower, and when you make male and female into a single one, so that the male shall not be male, and the female shall not be female. . . then you will enter the realm."

If Jesus was the bridegroom, then he and his family were responsible for the feast. This is why his mother sends the steward to him when the wine runs low. And yet, Jesus reacts as if he is not even a guest at the wedding, but a stranger. So why is he even there? And why does his mother seem to think that he's responsible for the wine?

In a Galilean marriage, the father would have provided the victuals, but no father is mentioned. In his absence, the son would be responsible for the feast, including the wine. The father is probably absent because he is God.

Given that the steward went to Jesus about the problem, the conclusion is clear: Jesus himself is the son, therefore bridegroom. But where is the bride? Who is she? We are not told.

In 591 or 592, Pope Gregory the Great declared that Mary Magdalene was a prostitute who had been forgiven and reformed by Jesus. It was not until 1969 that the Catholic Church finally acknowledged that there is no evidence in the gospels to indicate that she was anything other than something that they prefer to ignore, which was a disciple of Jesus and also a woman. She is never anywhere called an apostle, but she traveled for Jesus just as the men did. Her fate is unknown, but there are stories that she ended up after his death in southern Gaul, now the Languedoc in France.

Was she Jesus's wife, and is the story of the Marriage Feast at Cana the story of their wedding? There is no way to draw any definite conclusions beyond saying that there had to have been a bride and groom at a wedding feast, and, since Jesus was thought by his own mother to be in charge of the festivities and was not identified as the father of the groom, he must have been the groom. As to whether or not the bride was Mary of Magdala, we can only speculate.

In the place and time that Jesus lived, it would be surprising if a man was not married. Not impossible, of course, but marriage was considered so fundamental to Jewish life that an eligible bachelor in his late twenties would be unusual.

A fear of pleasure and of women is evident in much of the Old Testament and fills the synoptic gospels. Only in John is there a slight softening. And yet, as we shall see, the incident that initiates the passion is carried out by a woman of whom Jesus says, "Wherever the gospel is preached throughout the world," she will be remembered. (Mark 14: 9)

She is not named, though, and, as we shall see, this individual, who initiated the passion, has not been remembered at all.

There is only one place in all the Jesus material where a woman is given voice. The voice of this ghost, who may have been his bride at Cana, who may have given him the strength to undergo the passion itself, appears only in the Gospel of Mary.

The initial discovery of the Mary material was made in 1896 in a Coptic manuscript known as the Berlin Codex. Subsequently, additional discoveries have added some text to it, but it remains fragmentary. Some researchers have suggested that the Mary involved is Mary the Mother of Jesus, but most, I think correctly, associate it with Mary of Magdala. The first seven pages of all known copies of the document are removed, as are four in the middle of the book. In addition, the word that follows "he used to kiss her on the—" has been removed in all copies that we have. The pages may have been lost, of course, but it is odd that the same ones are missing in all the copies, and the removal of the word describing where he kissed her is obviously an intentional act, as it is done in the manuscripts themselves.

The Gospel of Mary was probably composed around 100 A.D., about the same time as the John gospel. The Mary gospel is explored in depth in Meggan Watterson's *Mary Magdalene Revealed* and Karen King's *The Gospel of Mary of Magdala*.

The suppression of this text was very thorough. It is not even listed among the apocryphal books in a list known as the Decree of Gelasius and attributed to Pope Gelasius, but probably of a later date. It sought to identify all such works in existence.

Of course, the primary reason for its suppression is that the creators of Christianity could not allow any hint that Jesus might have had a normal human life to enter into his *bios*, not if he was to be identified as God. A suggestion that he experienced sexuality would bring with it the assumption that he was human, and that could not—and in their minds cannot to this day—be allowed.

With regard to the Gospel of Mary, though, there is yet another reason, which is that it counsels an internal journey, rather than an external acceptance of doctrine. It also renders the ubiquitous "God the Father" of the canonical writings and most of the apocrypha simply as "the Good."

This desexualizing of God is almost unique in religious literature, and is one of the things that most sets Mary apart as a document of exceptional importance and value.

The gospel fell victim to the same effort to suppress *metanoia*, or inner search, that led to the destruction and concealment of the other important apocryphal texts. This can be seen clearly at the point in it where four pages are removed. Mary asks Jesus if someone who sees a vision sees it with the soul or the spirit. He answers that it is not seen with either, but rather with that which lies between the two, the *nous*. The rest of the text of the answer is missing. The Greek "*nous*" is usually translated as "mind," but for us that defines it as a brain function, which does not adequately reflect the ancient understanding. The Egyptians, for example, believed that thought originated in the heart. To the Greeks, *nous* is not mind as we understand it, but rather the more fundamental ability to see reality. *Nous* is the aspect of self that balances soul and spirit by understanding both. We now call this the intellect. In the Sphinx, it is the human head with its intellect, in the Trinity, the Holy Spirit with its mysterious spiritual power.

I think that the reason that the pages are gone is that they say that, when this balance is achieved, a person actually *becomes* their own Christ. This would have been anathema to the advocates of the Christ doctrine. We are not supposed to bear within us the holiness necessary to become Christ, but I think that this was the actual core of his teaching and the whole reason he was here in the first place. He was not saying to follow him. That was added by human authors who were creating a religion around his teachings. What he was saying, and I will develop this idea further in the next chapter, was to *become* him.

When he engaged in the ultimate miracle of resurrection, it was not something separate from his humanity, but rather an affirmation of the most profound human power, which has been locked away for all these millennia behind the mistaken belief that he was a god. We are like him in every respect, and his teaching was designed to help us guide ourselves deep enough into our own truth to see that. "Know thyself" not only means to know one's own personal psychology, but also to know the true power and enormous spiritual potential of one's own humanity.

When we discuss the Shroud of Turin, we will further explore the phenomenal consequences of the energies that are at play here. The brutal truth is that those lost pages of *Mary,* no matter how they got removed, even if much later and by simple thieves, have taken with them a great key to the reality and power of the human being.

The reason that I think that the life of Jesus must also have involved an actual, physical marriage is that it preaches transcendence, and that begins at the core of the person, where the blood is running and the nerves are singing. Transcendence cannot happen unless there is something to transcend, and that is what of us lives in the stream of time, and that is the body.

There is in Mary a sophisticated vision of an evolution of the human that transcends gender by melding male and female into one. This idea emerges later in the Tarot of Marseilles, which reveals, when laid out according to a very old but unwritten tradition, a path into the same genderless oneness that is the central theme of the Mary gospel.

The Tarot path is organized as a cross. The descending branch, the direction of the physical journey, starts with the card called the Lovers and ends with Death. The ascending branch, that of the spiritual journey, starts with the Magician and ends in the card called the World. It is numbered card 21, at position 22 (the card called the Fool is numbered 0). The World shows an entity ascending amid a wreath of honor. This entity is of ambiguous gender. It has breasts but its waist is covered in such a way that its genital sexuality is not revealed. At the four corners of the card are the four beasts of the Sphinx, indicating that the ascending being, who is genderless by combining both genders, is in internal balance.

The two into one is also addressed in the Thomas gospel: "Jesus said, "When you make the two into one you will become children of humanity . . ."" Here, as in other places in the Jesus material, wisdom is related to children and their innocence, rather than to sages and their knowledge.

A "perfect human" is spoken of in the Mary gospel. This

means one who is entirely devoted to the Good, which in the gospel is both the perfected state of the human being and the only name given to God. The Good is recognition of the needs of others, and marriage is a school designed to teach the partners how to do this. It is a constant struggle to understand the needs of others and put them before one's own. The great blessing, though, is to understand that your aim is not to look to your own needs but to those of your partner, and to learn to trust them to fulfill yours. This willingness to seek first for the needs of the other founds a great love. I don't think that it necessarily requires physically opposite sexes. Why would it? All it requires is honest love and the giving that goes with it.

While the Gospel of John is intended to refute Thomas because of the latter's advocacy of self-directed search, what John does in the case of the Mary gospel is to capture the women in it and place them near Jesus, but firmly outside of the ring of his trusted apostles, and certainly far from any suggestions of physical closeness and whisperings in the moonlight.

Unless there are two to begin with, they cannot evolve into a single one, internally surrendered both to the other and thus also to the deity who yearns to receive us all into the journey of the path, which is toward ecstasy, also called the inner realm, also heaven.

Of course, there is both an internal and an external marriage meant here. You cannot have a true story of a marriage without a bride and a groom—and no matter their genders. This is about an energy which does not rest in gender but in love itself. The story of the marriage feast has been edited to remove any suggestion that it might also have something to do with the ordinary love of man and woman, just as the Gospel of Mary has been edited to remove the touch of mouth to mouth.

Karen King's *The Gospel of Mary of Magdala* offers a nuanced translation and deeply reasoned analysis of the gospel which draws to the surface the struggle that Mediterranean cultures were having with femininity and pleasure. Her analysis of the difference between the Gospel of Thomas's "For every woman who will make herself male will enter the Kingdom of Heaven" and the Mary gospel's effort to describe humanity as fundamentally ungendered is revelatory, as is the gospel itself. In Mary, gender is part of the material realm, and the spirit knows no gender differences.

Mary, also, is announced in the gospel as a teacher of the other apostles, and, as King points out, there are many references in the canonical gospels to concepts that appear to be developed from Mary, or from the source that the Mary author used.

The harshness of human life in the Mediterranean Basin caused many cultures to fear that human pleasure angered the gods. In Jewish culture, this starts with Genesis and continues into the Christian era. In fact, it remains an enormous part of major Christian sects, most particularly Catholicism, which still retains a celibate clergy.

A great key to ascension that once lay within the Gospel of Mary and possibly also in a suppressed and now entirely unknown version of the Marriage Feast is that the path to heaven starts in the holy ground of the body. Ever since Mary and her wisdom were suppressed, Christians have regarded pleasure with suspicion, when the pleasure of the flesh is probably the closest a human being can come to experiencing the joys of heaven.

The Gospel of Mary reveals Jesus engaged in a partnership with a woman, knowledge of which, because it was probably physical and may well have involved marriage, has been completely eradicated from the record.

The lilies don't deny their nature, and neither should we, not if we expect to walk the path of Jesus. Our bodies, naked of hair, our already prominent genitals more to the front than those of any other creature, our sexuality knowing no season— all of these things have been given to us so that we can both explore ecstasy and create more human beings, and in so doing journey as far as life may take us along the sacred path of humble acceptance of the needs and potential of the body, which leads to the realm of heaven within, and the ascension of the soul.

8

MYSTERIOUS THOMAS

The Sayings Gospel of Thomas could easily be the most mysterious document in religious literature. In fact, it is so cryptic that many scholars have concluded that it has no overall meaning, and if you try to read it as we now read, as a narrative, that would be true. There are other ways of approaching it, though.

Along with other texts, it was discovered in 1947 in a clay pot in the sands of the desert near Nag Hammadi in Egypt. It was a small book, a codex, not much bigger than the palm of a hand. It is a list, or sayings book, consisting of 114 sayings organized in such a way that they can be memorized in groups connected by a single theme.

It has been called a gnostic gospel, but it is not quite that, for it does not follow the two central ideas of Gnosticism, which are a belief that we are in the thrall of a dark god, and that release comes from attaining relationship with a higher supreme deity.

When the gospel first appeared, probably as early as Mark, the complex Jewish religious culture of the period was absorbing ideas from the Greek community that had established itself in Palestine. From Jewish mysticism came the basic idea that influenced Gnosticism, which was that the supreme deity did not rule directly, but rather that man was subject to an intermediary who had brought evil into the world. From the Greeks came the idea that, since number must have preceded form, it must be the direct, sacred idea of the high God. This reflects the Egyptian idea that mathematics is both sacred and practical. Understanding number in its purest form, then, was gaining access to the mind of the high God—in other words, enlightenment, or gnosis.

Thomas is, in part, an effort to link the sayings of Jesus to the sacred mathematics of the divine mind. The sayings conceal an inner mathematical code, which is in part why they are often cryptic, even contradictory. Some of them appear to have been distorted so that the hidden code they contain will work. There is probably also another reason that some of them are so contradictory, at variance with the Beatitudes and even close to incomprehensible.

While Thomas is related to the canonical gospels, especially Mark, with which it shares twenty-one sayings, it is also connected to the ideas of Plato, and, more importantly to those of the Greek philosopher, mathematician and mystic, Pythagoras of Samos (570-495 B.C.) and the lost school that was based on his ideas. Its structure is based on prime numbers, which are numbers which can only be divided by themselves and 1. These were thought to be the purest and therefore most sacred numbers, and responsible for the structure of the world. Interestingly, the idea that math must precede form also has a place in modern scientific philosophy. In recent years, it has been explored by the physicist Max Tegmark in his book *Our Mathematical Universe.*

As is true of Jesus, there are no known texts actually written by Pythagoras. As is also true of Jesus, his ideas have had enormous influence. In and before the time of Jesus, they were foundational to Greek philosophical thought. While the crucial instruction to know oneself is, as we have seen, implicit in the Jesus teaching in the canonical gospels, it is directly present in the Thomas gospel, in Saying 3, which reads in part, "If you do not know yourselves, then you are poor, and that poverty is in you."

Rather than being a set of instructions, this gospel is designed to trigger revelations in the reader. Anybody who tries to view it through the logical conventions of modern writing will see chaos. In part, this is because of the way it approaches learning. In part, it is because of the hidden math.

The best book I have seen about that math is *The Thomas Code* by S. P. Laurie.

If you approach Thomas for instruction, it will defeat you. But if you try to learn from it, you will be rewarded. It is because of this approach that it was declared heretical by two church fathers, Hippolytus of Rome and Origen, a fiery defender of emerging Christian doctrine who was himself later declared a heretic. You can't find consistent doctrine in Thomas. In fact, if you are looking for "the word," it has little to offer but cryptic statements and contradictions...on the surface.

As to its date, it seems likely that it was written down by 60A.D. The first reason is that it contains a view of circumcision that is strikingly similar to the one Paul expresses in Romans 2:25—3:2. While Paul was preaching, the issue of whether or not an uncircumcised man could be considered a Christian was an important one. James, the brother of Jesus and the head of the movement in Palestine, was adamant that Jewish law had to be followed and physical circumcision was necessary. In Romans, Paul, who disdained circumcision, says, "So then, if those who are not circumcised keep the law's requirements, will they not be regarded as though they were circumcised?" In Thomas saying 53, Jesus is asked if circumcision is useful. He replies, "True, spiritual circumcision is useful in every respect."

Paul says that if men follow the law they will be "as though" circumcised, while in Thomas Jesus approves of "spiritual circumcision." The two ideas are very similar, suggesting this issue was relevant when both authors were writing. Later, of course, as Christianity became more definitely a gentile movement, its importance would fade. Around 60 A.D., though, it was very important indeed.

The second reason for an early date is the fact that twenty-one of those Thomas sayings are also present in the Mark gospel, suggesting that Mark's author was drawing on them. He may have known them from oral tradition, not from a written text, but he certainly knew them.

Just as John is the gospel of the believer, Thomas is the gospel of the searcher. John's Jesus says, "I am the way and the truth and the light," an unequivocal demand that he is to be followed without question because he is God. Thomas's Jesus says, "I am not your teacher. You are drunk with the waters of the flowing spring I have tended." (Saying 13)

What happens next is, if anything, even more remarkable. Jesus takes Thomas aside and tells him three secrets. When he returns to the others, they ask him what Jesus said. His reply is that if he told them, they would stone him to death.

This was the punishment for blasphemy, so it can be inferred that whatever Jesus said was so blasphemous that even his own disciples would stone somebody who repeated his words.

In the next saying, Jesus goes even further. "Fasting leads to sin. Pray, and you will be condemned. Give to charity and you harm your spirit." As if that wasn't enough, he continues, "When you travel about and people give you shelter, eat what they offer and heal their sick. What goes in your mouth won't contaminate you, rather, it's what comes out of it that will contaminate you."

His early followers, all Jews, are being told here that their dietary laws don't matter, but their preaching "contaminates" them.

Not quite the same idea as appears in Matthew 25:34—36: "I was hungry and you gave me food, I was thirsty and you gave me something to drink, I was a stranger and you welcomed me, I was naked and you gave me clothing, I was sick and you took care of me, I was in prison and you visited me."

Like much of the Thomas gospel, this seems an intentional affront to the core teaching. It would seem, then, that Thomas is attempting to discredit Jesus by putting words in his mouth that contradict his own teachings. But is this really true, or is something deeper unfolding?

I think what is happening is that the Jesus of the Thomas gospel is attempting to get his followers to see that they are acting and thinking in a mistaken way. They want to be believers, not searchers, and the Jesus of this gospel is deflecting their belief by forcing them to see it as absurd. If they call him 'teacher,' he reacts by sometimes teaching them rubbish and sometimes saying the opposite of what he means. Both things happen again and again in this gospel. What the gospel author is doing is forcing his readers to either swallow nonsense and contradiction or think for themselves. In other words, he is challenging them to search, that is, to let the Holy Spirit enter them. On the Jesus path, this always means the same thing: insight. The Holy Spirit is not some mystical presence—a dove descending from above—but rather, it's us. Our minds. When we use our minds to seek to know ourselves, we are engaging the Holy Spirit.

In this gospel, the disciples are looking at the path as an outer journey that will lead to an actual new kingdom in the physical world while the author's Jesus is advocating a new kind of kingdom entirely, which is neither physical nor spiritual, but rather is at once part of the inner life and part of the world. "The kingdom is inside you and outside you. When you know yourselves, then you will be known." (Saying 3) This means that self-knowledge involves a dropping of the border between oneself as a separate person and the larger "kingdom," which is at once a place of the spirit at large and of the individual heart.

As the Christian community grew, more and more different approaches to the ideas of Jesus appeared. By the late first century, for example, when John was written, there were many Jesus stories, and writing about him had become a publishing phenomenon, Roman-style.

The leaders of the Church, at that time a loose collection of bishops, began what would be a long struggle to replace all the theories and speculations with a consistent doctrine. Faith, which can be defined best, I think, as a confident yearning toward enlightenment, was being replaced by belief, which requires one to give up that quest in favor of accepted doctrine.

The trouble with belief is that there can be no final proof that doctrines are true. Because belief is a matter of pretending that something you cannot prove is, in fact, true, believers have only one defense: They must shout down those who disagree with them. Too often, murder becomes involved, even war. As we shall see, this is precisely the tragedy that befell Christianity just a few hundred years after Jesus was crucified.

The Thomas gospel is intentionally encoded to conceal its secrets from the casual reader while revealing them to the determined student.

In Saying 13, Jesus says "You are drunk from the spring I have tended." The next saying to mention drinking is 108: "Whoever drinks out of my mouth will become like me, and I shall be him." These two sayings, taken together, reveal that Thomas, (the name means "twin") has, after taking the message of Jesus to heart, become another version of him. That is to say, he has lost the identity he was born with and become another version of Jesus. The message is that our aim is to transform into our own versions of Jesus. To do this, a student of Jesus must act—that is to say, become one's own master. This is the exact opposite of the doctrinal thinking that John was advocating, where no search is necessary because the explanation has been handed down from higher authorities.

John identifies Thomas as the doubter in John 20:25, where Thomas is made to say, "Unless I see the nail marks in his hands and put my finger where the nails were, and put my hand into his side, I will not believe." Judging from how Thomas compels the reader to ask questions, it may well have been called the Gospel of the Twin to create doubt in the reader. A twin could have replaced him, could he not, and walked out of the tomb in his stead, thus faking the resurrection? The very name of the text is designed to force the student to question his teacher. But once the fallacy of that level of doubt is understood, then there is nothing left to do but ask ourselves, "then who is this twin?" It is us. We are Jesus's twins, all of us, male and female, and we are all capable of taking the journey of the passion, which is the journey of life.

This also illustrates the difference between the two ways of thinking in the two gospels, because the need to find literalistic proof is exactly what would not be important to the Thomas author. By the time John was writing, the Jesus path was already being submerged, its yearning toward the light and its inner struggle (*metanoia*) being replaced by exactly what the Jesus of Thomas scorns: himself as teacher.

As Thomas sees it, Jesus is something else, and very much more powerful: he is the instigator of the Holy Spirit. This is because he forces the seeker to ask questions, and to say of the gospel, 'What can it mean?' The instant that question arises, the Holy Spirit is acting on the seeker precisely as it did on Jesus when he was baptized—ironically by a very different John. "Just as Jesus was coming up out of the water, he saw heaven being torn open and the Spirit descending on him like a dove. And a voice came from heaven: "You are my son, whom I love; with you I am well pleased." (Mark 1: 9—11)

Jesus responds to this expression of love by letting the spirit take him into the desert, where he spends time seeking to understand his life aim. In other words, the Holy Spirit's action does not make him a believer, but a searcher. It is in the desert, alone and undisturbed, that he finds himself and therefore also the aim of his life.

Looming over the Thomas gospel is the shadow of a powerful mind, which is probably that of Jesus himself—an extraordinary genius capable of using his marvelous intellectual tools and his emotional conviction to instigate inner search in others by inexplicably contradicting his own teaching. Much like a Zen master, he disables the rational mind, catapulting the student into a state of perplexity out of which new insight can come.

This makes the gospel also a brilliant psychological ploy. It still works, too. The literature that has followed the discovery of the gospel in 1947 reflects a long struggle to understand. The gospel is not only a mathematical puzzle but a psychological machine that forces the reader to face questions he can neither ignore nor answer. This is why I think that it is an early gospel, and that it probably does contain some direct sayings of Jesus. In an era full of what we think of as superstition, being his student must have been a real challenge. It would be today—and, in fact, for anybody willing to face the challenge of Thomas, it still is. This teaching tool is very much alive.

If you try to use this gospel as a student would, to receive instruction, it is going to defeat you. Only when you wrestle with its mysteries will it prove rewarding.

There occurs in the gospel a saying, number 19, that refers cryptically to "five trees in Paradise." It's worth a careful look. The first sentence is, "Jesus said, 'Blessed is he who was before he came into being.'" This refers to entity prior to the existence of reality—to God before the universe existed. To say the least, it is an extremely sophisticated and subtle thought. It tells us that something existed before it *was*—that is to say, that the creator was potential before being. The next sentence is "If you should be my disciples and listen to my words, these stones will minister to you." The words are the stones. What he is saying here that if he is understood, then the teaching will enrich the listener. Indeed, an understatement!

The saying continues, "For you have five trees in Paradise which do not move summer and winter and their leaves do not fall." But why this specific number of trees, and what are they? If it is not randomly chosen, and that seems most unlikely, then it must be the key to the "understanding" that will turn the stones of the words into thoughts so powerful that "He who knows them will not taste death." That is to say, he will understand the meaning of this journey that we call life, and will see it in the larger context of being. He will know for certain that, as Dylan Thomas puts it so beautifully in his poem, "death shall have no dominion." Who knows the secret of the five trees in paradise will also know the secret of that which was before being existed—that is to say, what existed before it was.

What can that possibly be? Let's see if we can find out.

One characteristic of trees is that they are rooted in the earth, so these must also be rooted in something. They are not seasonal, though, but rather eternal. "He who knows them will not taste death."

Many authors have speculated about them. They have been identified as the Five Worlds of the Kabbalah: Atzilut, Beriah, Yetzila, Asiya, and Adam Kadmon. But the first written indications of the existence of Kabbalah do not appear until the twelfth century. Although its philosophy was probably in oral tradition before then, it seems doubtful that something so precise would have existed in an oral context with no written references to it whatsoever for a thousand years.

S.P. Laurie found his first clue to the Thomas Code in the Five Trees in Paradise. Typical of Thomas, the mathematical interpretation he discovered has nothing to do with the frequently proposed idea that they are the five senses, but still makes sense. This is because of the layering of the gospel. The mathematical, psychological and symbolic levels all exist simultaneously in the same text, but they neither intersect nor contradict one another. Whoever composed it was a breathtaking genius, which is why, again, I see the possibility that it is very close to the direct words of Jesus. This would also be why the terrible dark muscle that nearly strangled Christianity did what it did. . .but not quite. Like the Mary gospel and, as we shall see, the Turin Shroud, it has reappeared at the time when it is most needed and most likely to be understood. I will leave a detailed examination of the mathematical level to S.P. Laurie, as my primary goal here is to examine the other levels.

In the Acts of Thomas, a related text, there appears in Chapter 27 the sentence, "Come, elder of the five members of the mind, communicate with these young men." The five trees are mentioned in other gnostic texts as well. At the psychological level, I think that they are indeed the five senses, rooted in the body exactly as a tree is rooted in the earth. Unlike a tree, though, they are not seasonal, and they are indeed in the paradise of the body. Because it is so dense it is deeply embedded in time. We cannot see the future. For us, the next moment is always new, which means that, if we allow ourselves to notice this, we are always living in a state of wonder.

The Gospel of Thomas is a means of enabling the user who is alert to its hidden meanings to access insights that emerge as much out of the text as they are informed by the user's own understanding. I believe that the five trees are the axis of the gospel, which is about the journey of a human being into another state of being, which is "the realm."

Saying 19, after describing the five trees, concludes with the line, "Whoever knows about them will not taste death." This takes us back to Saying 1, "Whoever interprets these sayings correctly will not taste death." So the five trees are us, our bodies in life, drawing in all that we may obtain of the world— that is to say, the fuel we need to fire our search for self-knowledge.

For all its contradictions and mysteries, Thomas is, to my mind, the truest gospel, for it activates the energy that is the Holy Spirit of the Trinity and the intellect of the Sphinx in the searcher. When it inspires us to question its mystery, it also inspires us to face our own.

That is where the Jesus path begins, in the mind and in the word, in the fire of question.

9

THE PASSION PART ONE: TEMPORARY KING

There was almost certainly a teacher and political figure called Jesus, probably a carpenter, but just possibly a royal person, who died on a cross outside of Jerusalem. As we have seen throughout, there was and is also another Jesus, who is a vibrant archetype that seems to be touched by some mysterious level of consciousness that we might as well call divine. Almost as if it was copied from the past, his life contains eerie reflections not only of the life of Pythagoras, but also of those of the resurrection deities who came before him, gods such as Osiris, Adonis, Dionysus, and Mithra. The Jesus story probably touches history insofar as it retains at least the basic narrative of a real life, but the other Jesus, the one who lived in the teaching, has been buried beneath doctrine that can no longer feed our souls, and perhaps never really could lead us to the understanding that the Thomas and Mary gospels promise.

There is something about Jesus that is radically different from the other resurrection deities. First, he was almost certainly real—a simple carpenter, or somebody posing as such, who had absolutely startling insight into the life of the soul and the way of heaven. Second, the influence he has had in the world is greater than that of any other deity, philosopher, political leader—anybody at all. This apparent carpenter, who was probably illiterate and died as a criminal in an obscure corner of a forgotten empire, is the most influential human being who ever lived.

The resurrection gods are called scapegoats because they come forth and give their lives on behalf of the community. This is why their symbolic food is bread, the staff of life—why, for example, both Adonis and Jesus share the same symbolic birthplace, a cave near Bethlehem, the House of Bread. "Take and eat, for this is my body," said Jesus—an offering common, in one way or another, to all of the agricultural gods.

Only this was apparently not simply a story element, added after his death. What is so strange—and so very different—about the Jesus story is that he might have actually very intentionally enacted the ancient death and resurrection drama of the scapegoat gods in the real world.

There are things about his story that do not fit any current theory about him, not that he was god incarnate, not that he was an ordinary political revolutionary, none of the theories. To bring these things into focus is going to take detective work, and a dive into the deepest waters of spiritual search that exist, all the way back to our very earliest records of humanity's quest for truths that are eternal.

Unfortunately, when the emperor Constantine proclaimed himself a follower of Jesus as a god in October of 312 A.D., the old polytheism was violently rooted out. Its temples and books were destroyed and the age-old mystery cults that could have given us some clues to what the earlier resurrection gods meant to their worshipers were obliterated. The reason was that their ancient mystery cults were, as a number of non-Christian authors pointed out, very much like the Jesus story. The polytheistic believers accused the Christians of copying their mysteries, leading the Christians to brand them as demon-controlled.

After his crucifixion, a cult developed around Jesus that saw him as a mystery teacher who had become a solar deity. These were people, probably literate Jewish and Greek initiates, who wanted to use the life of this brilliant and passionate man as the foundation for a new version of the ages-old story of the scapegoat god, who gives up his life to gain divine forgiveness for his people, and rises again to lead them.

The reason they were moved to do this seems straightforward enough: there were evangelists crisscrossing the Roman Empire proclaiming that Jesus had been executed and then come back to life—literally. In other words, they were saying that the man had actually walked out of his tomb after being killed by the Romans. And they weren't just telling this story: they were on fire with zeal, shouting it out in the marketplaces of city after city, and they were convincing enough to inspire literate mystery initiates to write it down. To make sense of it, the Greek-speaking gospel authors told the story through the medium of a plot that they understood: that of the scapegoat god. They did this for two reasons: the first was that it fit the myth; the second was that—incredibly—it fit the facts.

Although there are few specific details of the old mysteries left, we can infer their content and intent from what was said about them. In Plato's dialog *Phaedrus,* for example, Socrates reflects on his own initiation in these words: "...we beheld the beatific vision and were initiated into a mystery which may be truly called most blessed, celebrated by us in our state of innocence." He describes those who have "begun the heavenward pilgrimage" as "living in the light." Similarly, in John, Jesus says "Whoever follows me will never walk in darkness, but will have the light of life." (John 8:12)

If Jesus had openly declared himself as an avatar of similar mysteries, the Jewish priesthood would have condemned him as apostate and possibly even hypocritically identified him as a Roman sympathizer—a fate he would certainly have wanted to avoid.

Judaism had well-developed mysteries of its own, but it was not primarily an initiatory religion like the cults of Dionysus and Mithra and Adonis, all of which were practiced in Palestine. (As we have seen, there is a connection between the Jesus story and the Adonis story. In fact, another reason for placing Jesus's birth in Bethlehem might have been to challenge the Adonis cult that was being practiced there.)

Like John the Baptist, Jesus also proclaimed that he had the right to forgive sins. To the temple priesthood, this was not only blasphemy, it threatened their livelihood.

Jesus certainly knew this, but he nevertheless abruptly left Galilee, where he had been safely outside of the notice of the Jerusalem authorities, and went to the city, their power center, where he would most certainly be noticed. He didn't need to be a prophet to predict what would happen.

Jesus, like all the sacred scapegoats who had come before him, was presenting himself to undergo his own initiation, which is to say, the destruction of his old life and his resurrection into the new. He was leaving the darkness of the material world and entering the light of heaven.

He arrived in Jerusalem on the same day, and possibly even at the same hour, that Pilate appeared coming up from Caesarea on the coast. The Roman governor normally lived in Caesarea, a new city, but during Passover he moved to Jerusalem in order to be available to quell unrest, which might well happen during the celebration of the Jews' escape into freedom, when they would have felt their submission to Rome most acutely.

Pilate would have come in through the Gennath gate and entered the Praetorium without venturing further into the city. He would have been accompanied by a magnificent guard of soldiers, some Roman, some Syrian, and some Jewish. They would have been carrying Roman Eagles, probably images of the emperor, and other symbols. As an image representing a god (Jupiter Best and Greatest), the eagle would have been particularly offensive to devout Jews and, as Pilate would have known very well, a disturbing suggestion—even, to some, a proof—that the Roman god was more powerful than Jehovah.

Jesus entered a gate that is now underground, beneath the current Eastern Gate. It was walled up by Suleiman the Magnificent in 1540 in order to prevent the Messiah of Jewish orthodoxy from appearing, as Jewish tradition had it that he would enter from the Mount of Olives through it—just as Jesus did.

Pilate rode a fine horse. Jesus rode either a colt or a donkey. Pilate would have been greeted by the assembled leaders of the city. Jesus was greeted by a raucous mob shouting his praises and covering his way with palm fronds. In other words, Jesus's entry was a parody of Pilate's. The avowed leader of the common people may have been lampooning the Roman prefect.

In a world where direct affronts like that were not at all well tolerated, Jesus must have been intentionally goading the authorities. But why would he?

There are three possible answers to this question.

First, he may have hoped for a popular uprising. If so, he would have been following in the footsteps of previous would-be saviors such as "The Egyptian" and Athronges, who had attempted to re-enact Moses' entry into Canaan. They did this as an act of sympathetic magic, in the hope of inducing Jehovah to favor their causes. But Jesus would have known that these previous efforts had failed, which could be why he chose a different approach. His sophisticated political skills and rich spiritual knowledge, put him on an entirely different level from the other "messiahs." The difference was his genius.

In addition to the followers who were with him, he had

helpers whose names and relationship to him are lost to history. Mark recounts that he said, "Go to the village ahead of you, and just as you enter it, you will find a colt tied there. . ." This almost certainly means that an advanced party unknown to the people who were with him had put the animal there. Jesus also warns them that people might ask why they are taking the colt, and instructs them to say that it will be returned. (Mark II: 2—6) Thus it would also seem that the local people were unaware of the advance party who had tethered the colt, and might think it was being stolen.

In the later gospels, the colt was changed to a "young donkey." John, who was most careful to make certain that the story he was telling fit the Old Testament messiah prophecies, put it this way: "It is written, 'Do not be afraid, Daughter of Zion, see your king is coming seated on the colt of a donkey.'" He is referring to Zechariah 9:9 which says "Thy king cometh unto thee, meek, and sitting upon an ass, and a colt the foal of an ass." Whoever had provided the colt may well have also organized the welcoming crowd and provided the palm fronds with which Jesus was greeted.

As Joseph of Arimathea, a member of the Pharisee class, later asked Pilate for Jesus's body and had it buried in a fine tomb, it can be inferred that at least some Pharisees were in the Jesus camp. Members of this class were wealthy and respected, and would have been able to organize a crowd, not to mention manage to get Pilate to allow an executed prisoner to be removed and buried. Normally, they were left on their crosses to rot.

After arriving in Judea, Jesus stopped in the town of Bethany outside of Jerusalem. It was here that the first incident took place that relates the passion story of Jesus to the passion stories of the earlier resurrection deities. "While he was in Bethany, reclining at table in the home of Simon the Leper, a woman came with an alabaster jar of pure nard. She broke the jar and poured the perfume on his head." (Mark 14:3)

What is happening is that Jesus is being prepared for burial while still alive, a common practice in scapegoating rituals. This would be followed by the flogging and derision of the victim, then his generally very painful execution. The word Christ, *chrio* in Greek, means "to anoint," coming as it does from the Egyptian word for mummy—*krst*, one anointed for death. When we call him "Christ," what we are actually saying is that he is dead to this world.

Interestingly, the only reaction by the people with him is to complain that the expensive oil (nard, from a plant in the Himalayas) has been wasted. Jesus responds, "She has done a beautiful thing to me." Then he adds, "She has poured perfume on my body in preparation for my burial." He then promises that she will be remembered forever.

The particular perfume that she used was among the most prized in the ancient world, an extremely rare oil with a soft and yet penetrating scent. When Jesus calls her act "a beautiful thing," he is saying that this unnamed initiate, but clearly one of high standing and great wealth, has afforded him an extraordinary honor. In that world, beautiful scents were equated with great souls, and nard was the most beautiful and rarest of them all. If Jesus was really no more than a revolutionary from Galilee, nobody was going to be anointing him with nard, no more than he was ever going to be noticed by upper-class Jews, let alone Pilate. He would have come into the city, perhaps shouted some threats against Rome and made some demands, then been dragged away by the first magistrate or soldier who happened along and promptly crucified.

If that is what happened, then this crucial moment was grafted on later, along with everything up to the crucifixion itself, in order to re-imagine him as a scapegoat god. But why pick this particular rabble rouser to be elevated as the Jewish competitor to divinities like Dionysus and Apollo? He was a country bumpkin, a Galilean and, as would have been assumed, not that much of a Jew.

If the incident—and the rest of the passion—actually happened, then the woman was an initiate into the mysteries that Jesus was enacting or she would not have known to do what she did. As the people around Jesus who spoke out against her had no understanding of her purpose, they were not initiates into what must have been a cult group of some kind—as it would seem, a most unusual one. Why I call it unusual is that it was supporting Jesus's effort to actually live the passion of the traditional scapegoat gods. As will be seen when we discuss the Shroud of Turin, whoever they were, they seem to have had truly extraordinary knowledge, as did Jesus.

As we saw when examining the story of the Marriage Feast at Cana, the canonical gospels are haunted documents. Just as someone seems to have been removed from that story, there is, at the beginning and the end of the passion story, a shadowy presence that is never directly addressed.

Somebody left the colt for Jesus to ride. Somebody assembled the crowd that met him. An unnamed but wealthy woman, or the servant of somebody wealthy, initiated his scapegoat journey. He says in Matthew, "Go into the city to a certain man and tell him, 'The Teacher says: My appointed time is near. I am going to celebrate the Passover with my disciples at your house.'" Matt. 26, 18—19). But who is this man? Obviously, he knows Jesus as a teacher, but he is not somebody who is spreading the teaching, not a disciple. So there were other people in the Jesus movement, in supporting roles, but who did not expose themselves publicly.

Another example may be the young man in the "linen garment" who flees from Gethsemane "leaving his garment behind." (Mark 14: 52) Is he in any way connected with the "young man dressed in a white robe" who the three women encountered at the tomb of Jesus? They are among a number of mysterious people involved in the whole affair of the passion, who appear to be orchestrating, managing, and overseeing things. In other words, Jesus was the visible element of a group who were helping him to enact an actual, flesh-and-blood version of an ancient symbolic ritual.

Some but not all of them could have been Essenes. The young man who fled Gethsemane wore linen and the one who was discovered sitting outside the tomb was clothed in a "white robe." According to Josephus in *The Antiquities of the Jews*, the Essenes were "clothed in white garments," and practiced a communal way of living similar to what developed in the Christian community of the first century. If Jesus was an Essene, he did not follow their custom when he allowed himself to be anointed with oil, for "they think that oil is a defilement." If the people who Mark reports as being present in Bethany when he was anointed were Essenes, then their anger at what the woman did is explained. But if Jesus's secret associates were Essenes, then who was the woman?

She was following in the footsteps of the goddess Isis, who anointed her brother Osiris before his murder. Was she, then, one of Jesus's sisters? If so, why was she wealthy? Or was the Nazareth story all along a subterfuge?

The others may be playing roles that were understood in the lost mysteries, but, while we know something about them from inscriptions and letters and a few general descriptions, the actual initiatory practices are lost. Scholars have speculated, of course, about connections between the various mystery cults and Christianity, but there can be no final answer. Even so, there are suggestive references. For example, the head of the Eleusinian mysteries was called the *hierophant*, or interpreter of the mysteries. Morton Smith, in his *Clement of Alexandria and a Secret Gospel of Mark* says that, in a letter from Clement to a correspondent called Theodore, Clement wrote that Peter, who gave his notes to Mark, "did not divulge what was not to be uttered, nor did he write down the hierophantic teaching of the Lord..."

Although it is, of course, possible that there were sacrificial deities during the hunter-gatherer era, the scapegoat gods as lords of fertility and rebirth probably emerged with agriculture, which would have been around 12,000 B.C. It would have been during this period, which was characterized by ferocious climatic and cosmic upheavals, that people began to have to grow edible plants to survive. As the great glaciers collapsed and the weather warmed, food animals moved away from established migratory routes, and many species became extinct. The animals and plants humans had fed on were disappearing. We know that the human population dropped precipitately. In North America, a massive fire, apparently caused by a large-scale impact event, devastated the continent, virtually destroying the human population. This was followed by a flood that covered much of the center of North America, caused by the rapid melt of the glacier that had stood across Canada and the northern United States for a hundred thousand years. This upheaval is memorialized in the geology of the continent by a formation known as the "black mat." It consists of a combination of ash and other material and is formed from the thick mass of debris from the fire that once floated on the flood that followed. It is found over significant areas of the continent, indicating the tremendous extent of the catastrophe.

The human population in North America was all but extinguished, and appears to have plummeted worldwide.

There is in the story of Isis and Osiris what may be a memory of this terrible era. In earliest times, the Egyptian story goes, the people were cannibals. Isis discovered wheat and barley growing wild, and Osiris introduced cultivation of these grains. The people then abandoned cannibalism and began to live as farmers.

In human societies, cannibalism usually emerges because of a lack of any other protein sources. If the situation is dire enough, tribal members will even consume their own relatives. This is because the survival instinct is more powerful than the most powerful taboo. So the story is probably a memory of a time when the population was so lacking in protein sources that the strong had to either cannibalize the weak or die with them.

The story of deliverance by Isis and Osiris memorializes the discovery of a way out of what must have been a dreadful predicament, a generations-long famine.

Once the Egyptians began to practice agriculture, they also attempted to control nature in order to ensure successful harvests. They used the only tool they knew, which was the sacrificial rituals that they created in their imaginations and offered up to imaginary gods—unless, of course, there is something about the relationship between man and nature which we in the modern world have lost sight of.

We know that both magic and sacrifice had been in use long before agriculture. This is because of the ritual chamber found in the Botswana cave, with its snake sculpture and ritually broken spearheads. There is no reason to suppose that this basic approach to controlling nature was any different in other hunter-gatherer societies. In fact, rituals still preserved in indigenous communities around the world reflect this same type of dual ritual practice—sacrifice accompanied by magic.

To gain the attention of the seasonal forces they sought to control, the Egyptians, like essentially all cultures at the same stage of development, personified the seasons the same way they had personified the spirits of the hunt, transforming them into deities so that they could be addressed with worship, to which they would hopefully respond with the gratitude of a good harvest.

While Jesus associated himself with bread like Osiris and

wine like Dionysus, there is a difference between the Jesus passion story and those of the scapegoat gods, and it is an enormous one, and very strange.

The earliest Osiris story, which appears on the walls of the Pyramid of Unas, is already a highly evolved myth. Rather than being strictly a fertility god, he is also there to help the soul of the pharaoh climb the ladder to heaven—the Ladder of Osiris, which was transformed in the Bible into Jacob's Ladder. Osiris is depicted with green skin, an acknowledgement of his role as the god of agriculture, also a predecessor to Jesus who, in John 20:15, is mistaken by Mary of Magdala for the gardener who tends the tomb. The Green Man as a symbol of fertility and rebirth appears in churches in northern Europe, where he was probably originally a fertility god who died and was reborn every season, like Osiris and Jesus.

Both James George Frazer in *The Golden Bough* and E. A. Wallis Budge in *Osiris and the Egyptian Resurrection* assert that Jesus and Osiris were the same deity, the essential god of the rebirth of nature.

I think that there is another way to look at it, which is that Jesus was *re-creating* the earlier passions, using the same theory of sympathetic magic that had inspired the would-be messiahs who had come before him to recreate the Moses entry into the Land of Canaan. Having seen that this method had failed, he was attempting another.

He did not try to re-create any particular scapegoat story, but rather evolved one that contained the essential elements common to them all: the arrival of the scapegoat at the place of sacrifice during the springtime, his humiliation and death by great suffering, and then his resurrection, and all of this managed from beginning to end by female adepts, chosen over males because they bear within their bodies the secret place of rebirth, the womb. Their attendance on him was another act of sympathetic magic, an attempt to engage the magic of the womb in his rebirth.

In the Egyptian mummification ritual, the body was anointed with fragrant oils that would both soften the skin and cover the odor of decay. According to Wallis Budge, the Egyptians did not believe that they were preserving the body for immortality. Instead, in their understanding, a nonphysical element that had gathered all the experiences of life was released from the body at death.

When a scapegoat god such as Osiris, who was the template for Dionysus and all the other scapegoat deities who followed, died, his soul remained intact and part of the physical world, a less dense but still physical presence so rich with spiritual energy that, at least for a time, it could be seen by physical beings and could interact with them. After touching them with fervor for the good, it ascended into higher realms where it fulfilled the duty for which it had been released, and pled the case of the people for admission into heaven.

We assume that Osiris never existed, or if he did, that he was not drawn up from death by his sister—as indeed, nobody can be restored to life after they are truly dead. Or can they? And I don't mean just metaphorically. What if there is something we are missing here—all of us, the believers, the agnostics, the atheists?

The gospels tell of a political life that leads to confrontation with Rome and a teaching life that in part involves an attack on the authority of the temple priesthood. But then there is also this other story, distinct from the other two, about an intentional march toward death that mimics the drama of the scapegoat gods. The stories of what Jesus did on entering Jerusalem and what he did in the temple are easy to accept as true. Was the woman with the nard a real person, engaging with Jesus in a mystical death ritual, or is she a later, fictional, addition? If she is, then her creation is part of an effort to identify the Jesus story with the ancient mystery religions. This would have been done to connect him to a gentile form of divinity since the Jews were rejecting the claim that he was a divinity in their religion.

I don't see how this question can be answered with finality, but judging from the way she appears in the story and her possession of such an extraordinary treasure as nard, combined with the fact that other wealthy people were working for Jesus behind the scenes, organizing his entry into Jerusalem and so forth, there is no compelling reason to reject the idea that she was a participant in the actual events that unfolded during the conclusion of his life.

As there was in those days no concept of separation between government and religion, and the government was an expression of the power of the gods, when Jesus acted against Rome he acted against its gods, and therefore his political actions were also religious actions. If Rome did not respond, its gods might become angry and punish the state. He was also standing up, as son of the Jewish god, to the Roman emperor, who was a descendant of the Roman gods and destined to rejoin them after death. He was saying that he was there to replace the divine Augustus, who was everywhere being worshiped as the ascended son of Apollo.

In other words, he was defying the Roman state and insulting its gods, and, for good measure, claiming that, as the son of Jehovah, he was above the Jewish priesthood.

All of these things were bound to lead to execution, which he had to know.

Was the outcome of this fury of defiance only that he died on the cross, or did something else happen?

At this point in the development of knowledge, that question can be addressed with greater depth and accuracy than ever before, if not yet answered in a final sense. The answers may soon be available, though, as we shall see. Even if they are uncovered, though, they will not put the mystery to rest. Far from it, they will lead to a new question, which will be the most provocative, universal, and also deeply personal one that has ever been asked of each of us, and of all of us.

It is this: who and what are we?

We assume that scapegoat stories are symbolic, not descriptions of actual events. There were never human beings called Osiris and Isis. Adonis was not born in the cave outside of Bethlehem and neither was Jesus. Dionysus never existed, no more than did Mithra. An angel didn't impregnate Mary nor a serpent Atia. Mary was probably the victim of what we would now call a rapist, possibly a soldier called Pantera, as Celsus claimed. Atia was made pregnant in the usual way, most likely by her husband Gaius Philippus.

Jesus was not a symbolic or archetypal figure, or not only that. Had there been no actual person, authors like Pliny and Tacitus and in particular Josephus would surely have written about him differently, if at all. They would have identified him as a heathen deity, not as a man pretending to divine status, which is what they did, and why they scorned him. At the time they were writing, he was assumed to have been human. Celsus, also, in providing him with a very human origin story, never questions that he was a real person who walked the Earth. Paul claims to have seen him.

And yet, the whole story—the anointing, the capture, the whipping, the humiliation, the terrible death and the triumphant reappearance—is to a greater or lesser degree present in the earlier resurrection myths as well. It is, in fact, the quintessential scapegoated divinity story, pared down to its terrifying essence.

I think that there is every reason to believe that Jesus actually lived the events described in the gospels. For one thing, looking back over the other stories, one does not find anything close to the sense of immediacy that is brought by the political element in the Jesus narrative. The earliest descriptions of

Osiris that we have do not paint a picture of him as a political figure, let alone a social revolutionary. He is a symbolic representation of both the human body and the grain. There isn't any suggestion that anybody thought of him as a real, flesh-and-blood person. People don't have green skin, for one thing. He and his sister and brother are very much personifications of natural forces.

This is true of the Jesus story, too, but it is embedded in a realistic tale that has the ring of truth about it.

From the evidence of the gospels, the Acts of the Apostles, and Paul, it must be said that Jesus created his passion. He intentionally took on the sins of the world, thus acting the part of the ritual scapegoat. But this is also, very clearly, a story of political-religious resistance. The other scapegoat stories do not possess this dimension, and this is what suggests to me that the Jesus story is true. This extraordinary man intentionally enacted the scapegoat ritual as an act of sympathetic magic. Astonishingly, as we shall see, there is significant evidence that it worked in ways that most of us now consider to be impossible.

To engage the power of the ritual the way he did, he and the hidden group who supported him must have understood it well. The followers mentioned in the gospel did not understand, and nowadays we reject it entirely. The resurrection, we tell ourselves, is just a story.

The power of what he did in those last days was so great that it overturned one civilization and started another one. It revised human morality. It instituted the idea that there is individual access to God. It was at every level the most profoundly revolutionary act in history.

Everything he did during his assault on Jerusalem has both political and religious significance. Everything is also a carefully staged re-enactment of the scapegoat god's journey to his death.

From the moment the unnamed woman poured the nard over his head, he was, like Osiris before his death, a corpse that was still walking, still breathing, but no longer alive. The living *krst*, already ritually mummified, now offers himself up for the sacrifice.

After spending the night in Bethany, Jesus entered Jerusalem, riding on the colt in ironic triumph. Pilate had the priests and the aristocrats. He had *his* people, the ordinary men and women who lived in debt and fear and hunger.

When he returned to the temple precinct on Tuesday morning, Jesus found himself confronted by a delegation of "chief priests, teachers of the law and the elders" who came to him and asked him by what authority he was "doing these things," which probably meant both entering the city the way he had and causing the disturbance in the Court of the Gentiles.

His response was typically brilliant. He says that he will ask them one question. If they answer him (he does not specify how), then he will reveal to them the source of his right to teach. He then asks them whether John's baptism is of human origin or from heaven.

They cannot answer either way. If they say it was of human origin, then they will infuriate the crowd, which is clearly very much with Jesus. But if they admit that it was from God, then they are hypocrites for their stance against him. So they cannot answer, and Jesus, therefore, doesn't need to answer them. He is not led into the trap they have set for him. Had he said his authority was from God, they could have accused him of blasphemy. Had he said it was not, then he could be dismissed. They lose that round.

He then tells them the parable of the murderous tenants, in which the tenants of a certain farmer kill all of the overseers the farmer sends them, finally even killing his son. The tenants are obviously hoping to steal the vineyard they have been paid to cultivate. In other words, they are acting out of greed.

If the vineyard is seen as Israel, then they are wicked helpers, defying God. They realize that "he had told this parable against them" and want to arrest him, but they are afraid of the crowd, and leave the scene. (Note that the crowd, which would have been a large one during this Passover week, is clearly on the side of the man it has welcomed into Jerusalem with such enthusiasm.)

There then occurs one of the great disasters of human history, which has led over the millennia that have followed to a vast amount of human suffering. It involves just twelve words spoken by Jesus: "Render unto Caesar what is Caesar's and unto God what is God's."

They are uttered in answer to the question of "some Pharisees and Herodians" who asked him, "Is it lawful to pay taxes to Caesar?" This is another trick, for if he says that it is, then the crowd will turn against him, but if he says no, he will be accused of sedition, a crime punishable by death.

Instead, he asks to see a coin. As the one they show him has Caesar's head on it, it is a Roman coin. Given that most Jews would not carry such a coin because it carries a graven image, they thus reveal themselves to the crowd to be allies of the Romans.

Jesus's response, "render unto Caesar," has been misinterpreted ever since. It has been used by kings and tyrants to justify keeping power to themselves. It has been justified by Christians, as it still is, to mean that they should obey the legally constituted authority without question. Many times, this has led people to accept misrule rather than face up to it, and to this day some Christian ministries teach that it requires them to always respect the established authority, no matter what they think of its morals.

Reza Aslan in *Zealot* points out that the word translated as "render," *apodidomi*, means "give back to." Jesus is not saying "pay Caesar," which is what "render" implies, but return the coin to him as it has his image on it and therefore is his coin. In other words, the interpretation that has caused so much suffering for so long misconstrues the statement. The next seven words, "give back to God what is God's," means that the land should be returned to God. (Remember that the Jews did not believe in land ownership. Israel was God's land. They were his tenants.)

So the statement actually means, "Return the denarius to its owner and return the land to its owner." As Aslan, I think correctly, points out, Jesus's statement reflects the agenda of the Zealot party, which was to re-establish the old customs when it came to the land, and remove it from the Roman control that was choking the life out of the common people.

Jesus had a political agenda, certainly, but there was much more than that, for he was also opening the door, by the actions he took during that Passover week, to the greatest mystery that exists. It is one which we are having, in our secular age, trouble even admitting. Christianity, trapped in doctrine that doesn't provide a key to the lock on that door, fails to open it as well.

Jesus had not said to respect the Roman government, but to give the Romans back their money and return the land to God —that is to say, send the Romans packing and live under God's law. This is the exact opposite of how the passage has been interpreted, and when we discuss Constantine and his linking of Christianity to the Roman government, we shall see why that has happened.

Jesus certainly knew what he was saying, and so did his listeners—the officials, the sympathetic crowd and undoubtedly whatever Roman spies had been sent to watch this potential troublemaker.

When he uttered those words, as he would have known very certainly, he nailed himself to his cross.

10

THE PASSION PART TWO: LIVING DEAD MAN

J esus committed suicide by crucifixion. There is no other way to explain his actions from the moment he decided to go to Jerusalem until the provocations he enacted there, carefully staged to guarantee that both the Jewish authorities and the Romans would want him dead.

His initial foray into Jerusalem was a provocation, but not a fatal one. The Romans didn't create history's most extensive empire because they were inflexible. Rather, they were generally tolerant of practically any belief as long as it didn't interrupt commerce or in some way insult their gods. They were less tolerant of sedition, of course, but there is nothing recorded about the celebration on Palm Sunday that would have concerned them enough to execute Jesus. He had not proposed to overthrow Roman rule. If he really was as popular as he appeared, Pontius Pilate might even have contemplated attempting to bring him into the imperial system and use his popularity to increase the stability of the province.

Jesus would have made a very different impression on the Jewish authorities. Just as Herod would have been afraid of a popular Jewish claimant being a temptation to Rome, the temple authorities would have been horrified at Jesus's popularity and afraid that Rome might overthrow them to take advantage of it.

He would have to work to get the Romans to execute him.

The gospels make him more a version of the scapegoat god than the Jewish messiah. If the passion story is even a reasonably accurate rendering of actual events, then, as I have said, it seems likely that he brought this about intentionally by doing what he did.

So what was his motive? Why was he so careful to identify his own passion with those of the other killed and resurrected gods, even though to do so meant that he had to make it even less like the messiah prophecies?

For example, nowhere in the Bible is there any requirement that the messiah die and be resurrected. This is not part of Jewish belief. Not only that, in Jewish belief, anybody "hung on a tree is under God's curse." (Deuteronomy 21:23). After his resurrection, Jesus tells his disciples, "It is written that the messiah would suffer and rise again on the third day." (Luke 24:44—46). But it isn't. There is no such statement anywhere in the Old Testament. So unless it appears in one of the lost books of the Bible (of which there are 33 mentioned by name in those that still exist), it is, simply, wrong.

But not when it comes to the scapegoat god. While crucifixion is not, despite an indifferently sourced book entitled *The World's Sixteen Crucified Saviors,* a form of death connected with these deities, the basic pattern of death and resurrection fits most of the gods whose stories reflect the seasons, as Jesus's does.

The birth of the solar deities who are also fertility gods is injected in their myths into the broader story of the death and birth of the plant world.

Jesus, said to have been born on December 25 and being called "the light of the world," reflects these traditions. There is no birth date mentioned in the New Testament. The tradition that he was born on December 25 probably arose as part of a Christian effort to replace the earlier deities. That birth date does not appear in the historical record until 336 A.D., when it is found recorded in a liturgical calendar

I have explored the idea that he intentionally set out to play the role of the scapegoat god. I think that this is further supported by the fact that the gospel writers have to contort his story in order make it fit messianic prophecy. He may himself have believed that taking the scapegoat role would also enable him to return to life and lead the Jewish people to freedom. But did he more than believe? Did he *know* this? As will be seen, this is actually a remarkably interesting question.

Jesus would have come up into the temple complex through the underground corridor that led into the Court of the Gentiles, a long *stoa* called the Chanuyos. It was designed on the Roman model by Herod's architects. This was where sacrificial animals were bought and sold, and where imperial coins that bore images of the emperor were exchanged for Tyrian shekels. Despite the fact that this coin not only displayed an image, but an image of the Graeco-Roman hero-god Herakles, it had been declared clean by the Jewish authorities on the rather flimsy theory that, since it was valid currency and not used for jewelry, it was acceptable.

When Jesus overturned the tables of the money changers, he was protesting against the use of this doubly blasphemous coin—not only was there an image on it, but Herakles could, under a strict theological interpretation, be thought of as a rival to Jehovah. But he was also interrupting commerce, and this would have been of immediate interest not only to the council who managed the temple and shared in its profits, but also to the Romans. Taxation under the early Roman imperium was not simply so that government could obtain enough money to run its bureaucracy and maintain the army; it was for the enrichment of the Romans and their city, most of whose citizens lived on an official dole and had no need to buy food. At this point in the evolution of the empire, subject peoples were not taxed as much as necessary, but as much as possible.

The odd thing about his actions in the Court of the Gentiles is that they were noticed at all. This was a huge public space, a long gallery that would have been, in this busiest of seasons, bursting with activity. So how is it that Jesus managed to create such a stir in this huge area that notice was taken? Not only that, why would he consider it sacrilegious that commerce was being carried out there? On the contrary, as it was where sacrificial animals were purchased for offering to Jehovah, this secular place had both a sacred and a commercial purpose, and it was both of them that Jesus was challenging.

By interrupting the flow of sacrificial animals to the Altar of Burnt Offerings in the Court of the Priests, he was blaspheming. By interrupting the flow of money, he was challenging the Romans. To make matters worse, and to make certain that there would be definite notice of his actions despite the fact that he must have been swallowed up in the crowd, he had entered the city the morning before in a triumphant procession, which ensured that the authorities would be well aware of his presence and watching his every move.

The scapegoat was ensnaring his own executioners in his scheme. But why was he doing it? What did he hope to accomplish?

For years, there has been debate about why he did it. He was acting against the priesthood, he was making a statement against blood sacrifice, against greed—the list is long.

Many of the scapegoat gods took on the transgressions of the entire community to deliver it from their consequences, and this is the core message of the gospels as well. "She will give birth to a son, and you are to give him the name Jesus because he will save his people from their sins" an angel tells

Joseph in Matthew 1:21. "Our old self was crucified with him so that the body ruled by sin might be done away with, that we should no longer be slaves to sin," explains Paul in Romans 6:6. And of course, Jesus describes the wine at the last supper as "the covenant poured out for many."

It is not possible to make a final determination about whether or not Jesus went to Jerusalem to set himself up as the scapegoat, or if this was grafted onto his life by Paul and the gospel writers. As I have said, there is reason to consider that it may have been an intentional act.

That Jesus went to Jerusalem, then got into trouble with the authorities and was executed seems likely, the reason being that not only the Christian authors but also Tacitus and Josephus make reference to his crucifixion. Tacitus reports that he "suffered the extreme penalty during the reign of Tiberius." In Book 18 of Josephus's *Antiquities of the Jews,* the crucifixion by Pilate is also mentioned. This passage contains some content that is probably a later addition, but scholars generally agree that the mention of the execution is authentic.

Jesus is portrayed in the gospels in much the same way that the solar and fertility deities are in their mysteries, but the stories of most of the earlier religions involve a god-man like Osiris and a goddess-woman like Isis. Aphrodite and Adonis were the couple in Syria, Persephone and Dionysus in Greece, Ishtar and Marduk in Mesopotamia, Magna Mater and Mithra in Persia, and in Judea Asherah and Baal.

While Jesus's story is related to these earlier myths, it is different in one crucially important respect: there is no female side to the couple. As we have seen, she existed and may even have been visible as his wife in a now-suppressed version of the Marriage Feast at Cana. She is certainly present in the Gospel of Mary. For the most part, though, in the Jesus literature she is a ghost.

After his anointing by the woman with the nard, Jesus

then goes back into Jerusalem, to the upper room that has been prepared for his final meal. As only bread and wine are mentioned, it is a ritual meal similar to those consumed in the various mystery religions. In 1 Corinthians, the magic of transubstantiation is implied but not stated directly. "Is not the bread we break a participation in the body of Christ?" Ten or fifteen years later, Mark is very specific. After breaking the bread, he has Jesus giving it to his disciples with the immortal words, "Take and eat: this is my body." Those seven words are the core of the ritual that enabled Christianity to develop into a world religion. This is because that ritual provides a direct link to deity that is more immediate than was the case in the older religions, which were seasonal. Jesus's annual journey through the seasons is reflected in the liturgical calendar, but his mysteries have been entirely detached from it, which is what separates his observance from all the other mystery religions, and gives it such power. You can commune with Jesus anywhere the communion ritual is being enacted.

After establishing this ritual, Jesus then retreats under cover of darkness to the countryside where he is hunted down by a group that appears to have been a mixture of Roman soldiers and agents of the temple authorities.

In a world lit only by flickering torches and dim oil lamps, this would not have been an easy feat, but they are assisted by Judas the betrayer, and Jesus is led to his trial.

If he was nothing more than a common carpenter with a loud voice, there was never a trial. He was simply condemned by a magistrate or perhaps a centurion, tortured as prescribed by law, and then crucified.

Whether this is what happened or not we cannot know, but we can know that Mark, writing thirty to forty years after the event, offers an elaborate narrative of a trial before no less a figure than the prefect himself, who would not have been involved even if Jesus had been a fairly prominent figure, and certainly would not have been called out at night.

Except for the very rich, the ancient world went to bed at sunset. They had to. Looking back from our world, which blazes with light, it is difficult to realize how very unusual such an elaborate nighttime operation would have been in those days.

And yet, this man was thought to be so important that not only was the prefect involved, he was involved at night. Moreover, a crowd was apparently present, because Pilate called on them to choose between Jesus bar-Josea and another revolutionary called Jesus bar-Abbas. Inexplicably, the crowd, whom the authorities have feared all week because of the popularity of Jesus, is now hostile to him, and they choose bar-Abbas— one of the most disastrous events in history. From the moment that this Jewish crowd cries out "crucify him" to the unspeakable horror of the Holocaust is an unbroken trail of blood measured not only in rivers but in two thousand grim years. No matter the twists and turns of history to which the ages-long persecution of the Jews may be ascribed, it starts with those two words.

But were they ever even uttered?

I am not the only person who takes an interest in this story to wonder who bar-Abbas was. Most scholars say that it means "Son of Abba." But Abba was not a last name, it was a familiar for "father," like, say, "daddy." So the name Jesus bar Abbas can be translated as Jesus, son of his dad, and it causes one to wonder, given that Jesus called God his *abba* when he was praying at Gethsemane, if perhaps there was only one man involved at the trial. Were Jesus the son of his father and Jesus the son of Joseph, in fact, the same person? If so, then the crowd was *not* hostile, and they wanted him released. They may even have been saying that they believed that he *was* the son of God, which the early Greek-speaking gospel writers like Mark have distorted because they were working from an oral source who did not know the meaning of the Aramaic *abba*. Either because of this mistake, or in an intentional attempt to blame the Jews instead of the Romans, it would seem that the gospel has been altered to make it appear that there were two different people involved, when actually the only one was Jesus himself.

The strongest suggestion that something happened other than what is recorded in the gospels comes from the fact that there was no custom of releasing a prisoner in honor of Passover. Surely, if this was actually practiced, it would have been mentioned at some point somewhere, for example in the exhaustive histories of Josephus. But there is nothing.

And then there is the improbable transformation of the Sadducees and their allies. Just hours before, "the teachers of the law were scheming to arrest Jesus secretly and kill him. "But not during the festival," they said, "or the people may riot." (Mark 14: 1—2) Then, that very night, they have a complete change of heart and arrest him after all—during the festival.

But what festival is Mark talking about? Surely it cannot be Passover. This is because the religious leaders themselves, as well as this supposed crowd, come out of their houses in the wee hours, despite the fact that Exodus 12:22 states that "None of you shall go out of the door of your house until morning," a rule that is observed all week. Also, Jesus breaks bread with his disciples on Thursday, not the day of the Seder, which would have been 15 Nisan which fell on the Friday. Until the Seder, the eating of bread was forbidden.

Either Mark simply doesn't know the Passover rules, or both Jesus and the authorities were breaking them. This is not impossible, of course, because Jesus was declaring a new covenant and, if he was as popular as he appears to have been, the authorities might have been desperate enough to arrest him even during Passover—and the fact that they did so at night would make sense, as most people would have been dutifully confining themselves to their houses, and the arrest of the popular rabble rouser could have been done secretly.

I think that the confusion in this narrative is further evidence that Mark was written in Rome and by a Hellenized Jew or even a gentile. He simply didn't know the Passover customs, and possibly wasn't aware that Jews locked themselves in their houses after dark during the festival. The later gospels attempt to correct the Passover error, and John finally solves the problem by removing the entire event from that week altogether.

As a Roman writing for Romans, Mark would have had a compelling motive to relieve Rome of the sin of killing a god, which would explain why he begins the process of blaming the Jews and absolving the Romans. As the Jews more and more rejected Jesus as messiah, this theme was elaborated on more fully in each succeeding gospel.

It is now sometime before dawn on Friday. The "crowd" has just agreed that Jesus bar Josea should be crucified. Unless they were part of the hidden group that was orchestrating the passion, the presence of that crowd makes no more sense than its hostility.

If they were somehow part of that group, or being led by its members, then they would have been playing a part in the sacrifice, and the actual double meaning of Jesus bar Josea and Jesus bar Abbas would be that Jesus the son of his human father was to die while Jesus the son of his heavenly father was to be spared.

But if the gospel was written for an audience in Rome, turning the Jews from approving followers into a hostile mob makes another kind of sense. At the time Mark was written, the empire was struggling at great expense to quell a Jewish revolution. Worse, Rome had just experienced a catastrophic fire and the emperor had burned numerous Christians to death in retaliation. The Christian community in Rome was in urgent need of two things: to separate themselves from the Judean Jews and to explain why they followed this new god from Judea. (The fire took place in 64 A.D., the revolt started in 68, and Mark was written around 70.) It is possible that the Jewish authorities had a hand in the execution of Jesus—indeed, likely—but the idea that the average person in beleaguered Jerusalem would scream for the execution of a rebel they loved the day before is extremely improbable. So, if there was a crowd, it would have consisted of the clients and slaves of the authorities, ordered out of their houses in spite of the hour, and not the common people.

As when we looked at the stories in the Infancy Gospel without the miracles, what emerged was a picture of a brilliant and troubled child, when we see the trial of Jesus as a secret affair, what emerges is a miserable little business where a brilliant man answers his accusers with skill and insight. Nevertheless, he is murdered by a prefect who one day would be removed from office after a formal complaint was lodged against him for crucifying so many people that his province was becoming ungovernably restless.

At his trial, Jesus is typically clever in his responses to his accusers. However, the one crime that he has committed against Rome—the one crime which, in Roman eyes, carried the penalty to which he was condemned—never comes up. He is accused of blasphemy, not of sedition which is why Pilate finally washes his hands of the whole affair and lets the "crowd" —or rather, the pro-Roman Jewish authorities and their retainers—have its way.

Pilate's statement that Jesus has committed no crime is there to ensure that the Romans will not look unkindly on the Jesus followers, and the hostile crowd is there to assure them that this Jew, not thought a criminal by the Romans, was hated by the very same Jews that the Romans themselves were coming to hate.

Jesus is now in the position of the scapegoat, but who put him there? If he did it himself, then he was condemned for sedition and that reality is not recorded in the gospels. But if they are a mix of fact and fiction designed to affirm his role as scapegoat deity, then he must be unjustly tried and must be despised by the mob and tortured and killed, all of it. And this is exactly what the gospels say happened. What was unfolding in the gospels, then, was that his story was being retold in a way that would appeal to Greek-speaking Hellenized Jews and gentiles who were firmly committed to Rome and who understood relationship with deity in terms of the traditional mystery religions, which held that a man who died and was resurrected became, like Osiris and the others, a god.

Having been condemned, Jesus is duly whipped. The *flagrum* was designed to rip the skin from the underlying tissue, chunk by chunk, with bone and metal bits worked into the leather thongs doing the damage. If hooks were added, the instrument was called a *scorpio*. The *flagrum* was also the symbol of the sun god (Greek Helios, Latin Sol) and appears on most coins that bear this deity's image. A typical example would display an image of Sol or the emperor on the coin's face, and the deity brandishing a whip on the obverse.

"The light of the world" (John 8:12) was a fierce flame indeed. As also occurs in the John verse, in the Orphic Hymn to Helios, the sun is described as "the light of life," and in some versions, "the light of the world." John's description is thus either an assimilation from the earlier religion, or Jesus was seen as the same entity as Helios.

But did the gospel writers intentionally identify Jesus with Helios or not?

There is a clue in gematria, which was invented in Babylon and used in Middle Eastern magic, then later also in Greek magic. Gematria involves assigning a number to a word based on the numbers of the letters it contains. It was intended to reveal the hidden meaning of words of power. It was also part of Jewish mysticism, so it is no surprise that the name given to Jesus in Matthew 1:21 is *Iesous*, "You will call him *Iesous* because he will save his people from their sins." Its gematric value is 888, which is the number of the Solar *Logos*. An unfortunate usage that has crept into biblical scholarship is translation of *logos* as "word." This started because it was translated into the Latin Bible as *verbum*, but that is not its Greek meaning. As the authors of the King James Bible worked from the Latin text, and the Latin *verbum* simply means "word," the real depth of *logos* has been lost to us. To even begin to grasp the meaning, for example, of the John gospel, it is essential to understand *logos* as the author would have. The primary meanings that would have concerned John were two: *harmony* and *principle*, which is how the word is used in the first line of the gospel: "In the beginning was the Principle, and the Principle was with God, and the Principle was God." When "word" is used in English, the sentence lacks clarity.

The "principle" here would be the mathematical unity of the universe, the celestial harmony that is the mind of God, which would be revealed in the gematria of the words of power. *Logos* can also be seen as harmony between extremes, the balancing intellect of the human head on the Sphinx and the reconciling force of the Holy Spirit in the Trinity. So the sentence can also read, "In the beginning was Harmony, and Harmony was with God, and Harmony was God."

A reader in ancient times would have seen a richness of meanings in that extraordinary sentence, which has been so tragically diminished in modern translations.

And so, we arrive here, in this holy place scattered with stinking corpses, the domain of carrion eaters and naked skulls, the destination of the *krst*, the living dead man. We are on a little hillside just past the walls of Jerusalem, high enough for all within the city to see us. Carrion birds wheel, feral dogs and rats swarm. Here and there, rotting corpses dangle from crosses. Masses of flies roar.

We have come to Golgotha, "the place of the skull."

Up a rocky path staggers a man. He is mostly naked. He is gasping. His hair is still matted with oil, his body exuding a stench of sweat and raw blood...and, faintly, the sweetness of nard.

Behind him comes another man, commandeered along the way to carry the cross beam that proved to be too heavy for him. He cannot die along the way. He must be seen there on that cross, seen by all.

Along the path, water has been left in a jar for the soldiers. Jesus, now a raw, bulging mass of broken skin and two anguished eyes, rushes toward it and drinks as much as he can before he is kicked away.

But why even bother to drink? It is for the same reason that he stumbled and had the *patibulum,* or crossbeam, taken from his shoulders. He knows that his strength is fading, and he also knows that, if he is to complete the mission that began with "Beloved are the poor, for they will reach the kingdom of God," it must end with the despairing cry, "*Eloi, eloi, lema sabacthani.*"

The cry is mentioned in Mark and Matthew, and took place at three.

He is laid out on the *patibulum*, nailed and roped to it by men who are indifferent to his roars of agony. And why would they not be? He's just another mad Jew, possessed by seditious ideas and aflame with hopes that, it is assumed, will die with him.

The crossbeam, with him dangling from it, is raised. It is affixed to the top of one of many vertical posts on the hill—as is said, between two others. As soon as the body dangles from the pole, as far as the Jews are concerned Jesus becomes cursed. There is now no possibility that this unclean man can ever be declared messiah. A final torment is visited upon him when his ankles are nailed to the vertical pole. This was done to prolong the victim's agony, so that he would be able to push himself up and draw breath.

He writhes and struggles. The flies swarm at him. The wheeling crows scream with excitement. A distance down the hill, some women bear witness, weeping and mourning, their tears expressing a sorrow that has lived on and on and on, down all these ages from then to now.

From noon, there had apparently been a dust storm blowing. "At noon, darkness came over the whole land until three in the afternoon." These were and are common in the region, and blow in the area in spring and fall. The Egyptians call them *khamsin*, and in Hebrew they are called *ruah kadim*, the "east wind." They can be absolutely suffocating and completely block out the sun.

By three, the dust storm would still have been raging. Jesus would have been suffering now for hours in the blinding half light, feeling his strength wane, and it is now that he utters the haunting cry that is traditionally connected to Psalm 22:1: "My God, my God, why have you forsaken me?"

But which god? Mark has it that he said, "*eloi, eloi, lema sabacthani.*" Matthew has "*eli, eli.*" But, as is pointed out in the Jerusalem Bible, if he had meant "my God," he would have said "*ilahi.*" Among Greek speakers, *Eli* was the name of Helios, the sun god. So was he calling to the sun, asking why he had been abandoned by the light? Did he call from the cross on the sun to save him, and is that why, after his resurrection, his story became entangled with those of the others who had been killed and resurrected as solar deities?

Perhaps so, but there is a larger question here. Why has he thrown away his crucially important teaching ministry in favor of this humiliating martyrdom? There is only one reason, and it involves a great secret, which is the truth about light.

11

THE STRANGEST THING IN THE WORLD

The journey of Jesus does not end on the cross. That's where it begins.

At first, it must have seemed that he was just another zealot who tried to defy the Romans. He made grand promises that he failed to keep. The Jews had seen it all before —the inspiring claims, the dramatic miracles and the ignominious defeat at the hands of the Romans.

But from the beginning of this book, there has been a persistent question: why would his followers, instead of dispersing like those of all the other failed messiahs of the era, go marching out into the world spreading his message?

The reason is very simple: starting a few days after he was laid in his tomb, an event happened so inspiring that it motivated them not only to stake their lives on it, but to give them up for it.

These were not rich and powerful people, they were carpenters and fishermen and farmers, illiterate men and women of the lowest rank. Such people are normally silenced by the burden of their lives, but these *tektons* and laborers and fishermen and seamstresses and weavers inexplicably gained their voices and began to shout up and down the creation that a dead man had come back to life and mankind was redeemed.

In Judaism, every word of it was blasphemy. Their ignorant story didn't fit the prophecies of the messiah. And as far as the gentiles were concerned, they already had Osiris and Dionysus and Adonis and all the others. What did they need with a new scapegoat god, and not only that, one that these ignorant louts were claiming had *really* risen from the dead, not like in the mysteries, where it was all theater?

These people had gone mad, clearly.

Or had they?

In the mid1970s, Anne and I were invited to a talk in New York that was given by Father Peter Rinaldi on the Shroud of Turin. He introduced the Shroud of Turin Research Project (STURP), which was just then getting underway. Father Rinaldi was helping raise funds for the project. Prior to meeting him, neither of us had been much aware of the Shroud. As we rode home in a cab afterward, I asked Anne what she thought. When she remained silent, I said, "I think it's real." She replied, "I was afraid you'd laugh at me, but I do, too."

We didn't have a lot of money, but we contributed, as I recall, a thousand dollars, and from time to time after that got progress reports, which were very impressive, and so was the final report produced by STURP.

We were pretty well convinced that the Shroud was something very extraordinary. But what? We were at a loss.

It was in 1988 that we heard an NPR reporter convey the news that the Shroud had been definitively dated to the early Middle Ages. By then, we had been studying the Shroud literature for years, and knew enough to understand that this was a very unexpected finding.

Not only was Dr. Harry Gove, who was the *de facto* leader of the carbon dating team, the inventor of the mass spectrometry carbon dating method that was used to do the dating; the protocols that had been followed appeared to have been developed to a high degree of professional finish. When I read the report of the findings, which was published in the prestigious scientific journal *Nature* in 1989, I was left thinking that great care had been taken. I was disappointed, but also suspicious. Anne was more than suspicious. She said, "They got it wrong."

She said this because some of the earlier research spoke so convincingly in favor of the cloth being an anomaly. Since 1988 there has been more research—much more, in fact—and many of the findings are not just strange, they are spectacularly so.

The Shroud is not a medieval forgery. In fact, if we set out to forge it right now, we couldn't do it. We couldn't even come close. Nevertheless, after the 1988 findings were released, the Shroud story died away. To this day, when I bring it up with most people, the reaction is that it was proved to be a forgery.

The first time it was ever called that was in 1390, when Bishop Pierre d'Arcis wrote Pope Clement calling it a "clever sleight of hand." He claimed to know the artist who had created it, but never produced this person. It developed that the bishop's diocese was being bypassed by pilgrims intent on seeing the Shroud, which was in a church is a neighboring diocese. The bishop complained to the pope, "The Dean of a certain collegiate church, to wit, that of Liery, falsely and deceitfully, being consumed with the passion of avarice," had procured the Shroud for his church and was charging admission to see it.

In 2018, Drs. Matteo Borrini and Luigi Garlaschelli used a living volunteer and real and synthetic blood to try to simulate ways that the bloodstains could have gotten onto the Shroud. (For a long time, scientists were sure that these were blobs of paint, but testing had by then confirmed that it is human blood.) They concluded that two rivulets of blood on the left hand were consistent with somebody holding their arms up in a "Y" while standing over the cloth. But if the stains were transferred from the hand of a man who had been hanging from a cross, the result would have been the same.

The findings, published in the *Journal of Forensic Science*, concluded that the stains seem to have fallen from somebody standing vertically rather than lying in the cloth. The actual reason that the blood marks (they are not conventional blood-stains) are positioned where they are, however, is much stranger than that.

Because there is no way to know how the body was handled while it was being wrapped in the Shroud, the Borrini/Gar-laschelli study must be said to be inconclusive, except insofar as it did confirm that, while the blood was running down the left arm, it was raised exactly as it would have been if the man was on a cross.

There are many problems with the 1988 carbon dating, as Mark Antonacci discusses in his books *The Resurrection of the Shroud* and *Test the Shroud*. Research done since 1988 has shown why the carbon dating results must be inaccurate.

Dr. Gove, as he makes clear in his 1996 book *Relic, Icon or Hoax: Dating the Turin Shroud*, came to the project with a deter-mination to prevent the Shroud of Turin Research Project scientists from being involved in any way at all. This was inten-tional, because with his knowledge of the strengths and weak-nesses of the carbon dating method he himself invented, he appears to have wanted to make very sure to take cloth samples from the Shroud for dating from areas that would be the ones most likely to provide inaccurate data.

In his book, he describes how he was able to prevent STURP from playing any role in selecting the samples. This would have been because STURP had maintained that samples should be removed from several different areas, and areas that contained scorch marks, water marks, repairs or other contami-nation should have been avoided. Instead, with STURP out of the way, Gove made sure that only one sample was taken, and as Mark Antonacci says in *Test The Shroud,* "it was from the worst possible location on the entire cloth." That Dr. Gove would not have understood this very clearly is most unlikely. If Antonacci is right, it must be concluded that Gove's objective was not to date the cloth, but to make sure that the latest possible date was obtained.

In the presence of the directors of the three laboratories that would test the samples, a 285 milligram piece of cloth (far more than necessary) was cut out of the edge of the main portion of the Shroud and given to the laboratories in Tucson, Zurich, and Oxford. The three samples were located about 18 inches from the image of the body, and ran parallel with it around the ankle. If the samples were uncontaminated or unaffected by other forces (more on that later), they should have returned consistent dates. But instead, the samples which were closest to the image of the body returned dates that were younger than the samples farther from it. This indicates that some outside factor must have been at work on the cloth, either contamination or some other process that affected the amount of carbon-14 in the fibers. Instead of revealing this, the coordinators at the British Museum basically massaged the data by combining their ages and eliminating the youngest datings from the report. This effectively prevented a conclusion that the data might not be consistent enough to make a determination. So the project was hardly handled at the high degree of professional finish that the media made it appear.

Harvard physicist Dr. Thomas Phillips makes the point in a comment on the *Nature* article published on February 16, 1989 that "...the image on the Shroud, which still cannot be duplicated, appears to be a scorch, indicating that the body radiated light and/or heat. It may also have radiated neutrons, which would have irradiated the Shroud and changed some of the nuclei to different isotopes by neutron capture. In particular, some C^{14} could have been generated from the C^{13}. If we assume that the Shroud is 1,950 years old and that the neutrons were emitted thermally, then an integrated flux of 2×10^{16} neutrons/cm-^{2} would have converted enough C^{14} to give an apparent carbon-dated age of 670 years." He further points out that, if this happened, the amount of C^{14} would have differed in different parts of the Shroud, which is exactly what the raw data showed.

Of course, the other scientists disagreed with this entirely. One of them, Dr. Robert Hedges from the Oxford lab, offered the opinion that it "beggars scientific credulity." However, the image on the Shroud, even then, was known to be some sort of scorch mark, and a very strange one indeed. Therefore, what *does* beggar scientific credulity is the idea that an accurate dating can be arrived at using the carbon dating method that was applied. In order to even know whether or not carbon dating is an appropriate test, much more must be understood about the image, the nature of the energy that created it, and the ways in which that energy might have altered the nuclear structure of the cloth.

Nevertheless, the report was submitted to the world and the media quite naturally followed lead of the scientific authorities in dismissing the Shroud. For example, in the Peter Jennings report *Still Shrouded in Mystery,* in 1988, Dr. Edward Hall of Oxford called the idea that there was anything unusual about the image "a load of rubbish."

The reason for all this hostility is the fear that, if the Shroud is indeed inexplicable and shows what it appears to show, then there is an enormous hole in the basic materialist paradigm. It means, at the most fundamental level, that we do not know how reality works. Moreover, if you admit that the cloth does contain an image that was generated by the body that was lying in it, then miraculous intervention seems to be the only way to explain it.

I don't think so. I don't think miracles can occur. As I have indicated before, I think that there are probably accounted for by natural phenomena that we have not yet understood. We forget all too easily that reality doesn't necessarily end at the limits of our understanding.

As we shall see, the vehemence of the Shroud deniers stems from two very deep parts of human nature: our need to believe and our fear that our beliefs may be unfounded. We want desperately to make sense of the world, and as I have pointed out before, we are willing to defend our beliefs to the death— preferably of those who disagree with us.

The idea that the Shroud might be a genuinely anomalous relic is particularly threatening to the scientific community. Science endured over a thousand years of religious repression, and the idea that the Shroud, if proved authentic, might validate the doctrinal orthodoxy that sent a genius like Giordono Bruno to the stake and very nearly did the same to Galileo, is absolutely terrifying.

I don't blame them. The repression of the intellect in the West lasted from the promulgation of the Nicene Creed in 325 and 381 A.D. until the rediscovery of Lucretius' lost epic of secular Epicurean philosophy, *On the Nature of Things* in 1417 by Poggio Braccolini in a Benedictine abbey in Germany. The agonizing crawl from there to the High Renaissance and finally the Enlightenment and with it, at last, the collapse of the religious dictatorship, was a slow, dangerous and uncertain affair. This fear emerged into the Shroud project when Dr. Gove, working tirelessly to make certain that the STURP scientists were allowed to play no role in the carbon dating, characterized them as religious fanatics. He believed this and feared that anything except a complete dismissal of the mystery would lead to their proclaiming, as scientists, that the Shroud was proof that the resurrection had really happened and further that Christian doctrine as set out in the Nicene Creed was literally true.

Those were the lines: secularism versus religion. One side maintained that Jesus was just a man who died on a cross, and nobody was required to believe in his divinity or, in fact, in any god. The other maintained that he walked out of his tomb alive again and therefore was God, and thus that Christian doctrine as established at the Council of Nicea had better be followed to the letter.

The secular believers are wrong about the actions and afterlife of Jesus. As we have seen, he was indeed a miracle worker, but the miracles were not supernatural, but caused by natural forces that remain to this day little understood, but which he did understand, at least well enough to make use of them.

As we shall shortly see, he almost certainly did have a truly remarkable afterlife, but again, not due to the arbitrary injection of a miracle. Rather, it was caused by the action of human power that apparently results in the transformation of a physical being into a form of highly energetic conscious light.

We don't know what this is, and certainly not what, if anything, it has to do with religious doctrine that was created to explain it thousands of years ago. So, unless the Shroud advocates really are fanatics who have promulgated a massive fraud, the Shroud is an artifact of a form of energetic transformation that we do not understand. It is not proof of religious doctrine. All that can be said of it is that something happened to the body that it contained that caused the effects that were observed.

The god who demands blind belief and is called Christ is not Jesus the teacher, but a later invention. The Gospel of Thomas reveals the real Jesus in his truth, I think, as a teacher so courageous and so intent on challenging his students that he will deny his own teachings in order to make them think for themselves.

The gospel accounts, with their references to the traditions of the solar deities, reflect an attempt to make sense of something that looked to the people of the time as if a god from a mystery religion had actually returned to physical life. And yet he was a Jew, or at least a Galilean, and not apparently connected to the familiar solar deities. In their attempt to understand, they plucked from the only knowledge trees they possessed at the time, which were the messiah prophecy and the stories of the solar deities.

This may be why Paul chose to preach his version of the Jesus story as a simulation of Mithraism. He had no other way to describe what had happened, and no other way to characterize Jesus except in terms that he and his peers understood.

Mark, in its earliest version, only mentions that Jesus was gone from the tomb, and omits the verses about him appearing to Mary Magdalene and then to others that are present in later manuscripts. The other gospel that may be very early, Thomas, doesn't mention the resurrection, either.

There may be a reason for this other than the assumption made by the secular scholars, which is that Jesus didn't appear to anybody because he was dead. The reason that Mark didn't report the appearances, which must have been prominent in the oral narrative, could have been that they were considered secret at the time. There could have been two reasons for this: the first might have been that Mark assumed that the resurrection story meant that Jesus had survived the crucifixion by something other than miraculous means, and therefore that he might still be alive and in hiding. The second would have been that the suspicion that he had survived, even if untrue, might cause the Romans to investigate. They would have tortured his friends and family in an effort to find him. This could easily have ended with the destruction of the entire movement. After all, when Mark was writing, the burning of the Christians of Rome and the destruction of Jerusalem and the temple were current events.

It's not impossible that Jesus could have performed a magic

effect on the cross. In fact, the various tricks involved in seemingly bringing the dead back to life must have been known to many people in the ancient world, given that this is one of the most commonly described magical feats, and one which Jesus himself frequently performed.

How might it have worked, though? It might be that Mark tells us. "With a loud cry Jesus breathed his last." (Mark 15:37) He would have then slumped down and become still. The flies, which would have been rising in a cloud every time he pushed himself up to breathe, would have settled like a gray shroud over his body, energized by the raw blood from his scourge marks.

The next thing that happens is that somebody "ran and filled a sponge with vinegar." Was this one of his mysterious helpers, and was there something other than vinegar on the sponge? Opium preparations were known at the time. They are mentioned in Egyptian texts, and Galen describes their use to induce anesthesia. If he had ingested a powerful opium draught and not vinegar at all, nobody would have doubted that he had died.

Note that, when Joseph of Arimathea went to Pilate to request the body be given to him, Pilate was so unsure that Jesus was really dead that he sent a soldier to check on him. The reason was that they had refrained from breaking Jesus's legs, undoubtedly to prolong his death and make it more of a spectacle. And yet here he was, supposedly dead before the end of the first day. Pilate had probably anticipated that the city would watch Jesus writhe and groan at least through the next day.

Nobody would have doubted that he was dead. . . until the women found the tomb opened. The young man who greeted them told them only that, "he is risen," and there the Mark gospel ended until around a hundred years after it had been written. By that time, of course, there could be no further danger to Jesus. But in the years immediately following the event, people like Mark, who had not witnessed any of the events and was writing in faraway Rome, might well have suspected that the great teacher had survived the crucifixion by trickery and was a fugitive.

Logical enough, but inconsistent with the reactions of the people who are reported to have actually seen him. For the rest of their lives, they lived for his teaching—and they died for it, one apostle after another.

So how was the Shroud created, and when?

I have called it the strangest thing in the world because that's exactly what it is.

12

THE RESURRECTION IN REALITY

A wealth of evidence has been amassed since the 1988 tests that makes a powerful case for the assertion that the image on the Shroud was created by unknown means and cannot be duplicated even now, and could not have been a medieval forgery.

In this chapter, I will discuss some of the highlights of this work, and the extraordinary mystery that has been uncovered.

At this point, though, I must say that I did not expect this outcome. I am comfortable with the idea of an afterlife. My book *the Afterlife Revolution* explains why. I have had much personal experience of a nonphysical aspect of the human being, as discussed in the book I wrote with Dr. Jeffrey Kripal, *Super Natural*. But this—that a body could dematerialize and reform as an entity of light—I find just terribly improbable.

And yet, as shall be seen, there does not appear to be another explanation.

First, analysis of the image has revealed that the individual who left it behind was scourged, carried a heavy object across his shoulders, had nails driven through his wrists and ankles, was pierced in the flank after death, and died of asphyxiation.

So if that man was indeed Jesus of Nazareth, then there was no trickery involved on Golgotha. He died as a result of crucifixion.

If there was trickery involved in the creation of the image, it was carried out by the use of processes that are completely unknown to us. As we shall see, it cannot be a medieval forgery or a natural effect of any known kind, and it cannot be produced now.

Among other things, the condition of the cloth has enabled measurement of the energy needed to generate the image, and that amount of energy could not be produced in the short time that it took for it to be imprinted on the cloth, not in the past and not now. We could not re-create the Shroud today, which would be why the various attempts to do so using lenses and various light sources have not produced anything even close to the detailed image that appears on it.

No other piece of cloth, either burial cloth or otherwise, has ever been found that displays an image like it.

Additionally, a body of forensic evidence has been gathered over the past twenty years that shows that the cloth was at one time not only in Palestine, but actually near Jerusalem, and that its subsequent movements, revealed by pollens and other debris left on it, closely follow the path that legend has it that it followed in its long journey from the tomb of Jesus to its present resting place in Turin Cathedral.

I find it interesting, also, that, like the gospels of Mary and Thomas, so crucial to a new vision of Jesus, this evidence has emerged at this particular time in the life of the world. We are at a point of reckoning, and these three things together—the two gospels and the Shroud—are revealing secrets that are going to enable us to understand not only this courageous and holy man, but ourselves, in an entirely new and much richer way.

Just when we need these tools, here they are.

As we have seen, Jesus was no ordinary person. So was he, then, a divine figure separated from us by a fundamentally different and higher nature?

In the next chapter, I will explore how it came to be believed that he was just that, and also why there is more to the story.

What we can do now is look past the confusion that arose when the gospel writers attempted to explain something that they could not understand, and examine using modern scientific analysis what happened to the Shroud of Turin.

First, the image is not an artwork. It is also not a photographic image. While some elements of it may have been producible by artistic or photographic techniques, the image itself cannot presently be reproduced.

The simple reason for this has been obvious for years. Because what it means is so devastating to the way we have come to see the world, as essentially an interplay of material and energy that can be understood by applying established laws of math and physics, we have been denying it right along. This was well known before the 1988 dating that debunked the Shroud. It is because the perspectives displayed by the image mean that it must have been created by some energy that radiated outward from inside the cloth.

We know this because, when it is rendered into three dimensions, it becomes clear that the image's shadings could not have caused light shining on the body's contours from the outside, as is the case in photography. They could only be caused because the distance of the various body parts from the cloth meant that slightly different energy intensities reached it, depending on how far each body part was from the cloth when the radiation event took place.

This effect was discovered by physicist and STURP cofounder John Jackson and image specialist Bill Mottern in 1976. Thus, the Shroud image was not produced by a method like photography. It was also not produced by a lens-and-mirror system such as the one that artist David Hockney theorizes in his book *Secret Knowledge* was in use by artists during the Renaissance, and with which he believes the old masters produced their ultra-realistic paintings.

It was also not caused by some sort of rare chemical effect. This, also, would have generated an image with the same dimensional properties as a photograph. The energy that created the image emanated from the body, impacting the cloth with different levels of intensity depending on how far a given area of the body was from the cloth. Judging from the detail involved, this energy must have consisted of very short waves. The fact that only the surface layer of cellulose in the fibers was affected means that the energy burst was extremely brief.

When the event that left the image behind happened, the man had been dead for perhaps 48 hours, but probably not more than 72 hours. This is because the effects of rigor mortis are visibly present in the body image in various places, including the thighs, buttocks, torso, thumb, and left leg. There is postmortem blood and fluid flow from the flank wound, and the condition of that wound indicates that it was inflicted after death.

The absence of any further signs of dissolution in the form of fluid stains on the cloth due to later settling of the body means that after the image was formed, the body ceased to be present in the Shroud. While there is no scientific explanation for how such an energy burst could have been produced, its intensity has been measured by examining the marks on the cloth that form the image. That some kind of very brief radiation burst was involved is suggested by the fact that only the surface fibers of the threads are affected. Not only that, the great detail that is present is due to the fact that individual fibers were affected differently as the radiation passed through them, meaning that its level of intensity varied minutely, from fiber to fiber.

The cloth is woven in a 3:1 herringbone pattern and spun with a Z twist. It's a complex weave, and, while it was a high—quality piece of cloth for the time, it was not unique. There are examples dating from well before the first century. For example, a late Bronze Age cloak found in Germany was woven with the same 3:1 herringbone pattern, and even more sophisticated weaves are found in Egypt. The linen girdle of Ramses III (1200 B.C.) is woven with threads of five colors with a 3:1 twill alternating with a 4:1 and 5:1 weave, and these are just two examples. Also, according to Dr. Mechtild Flury-Lemberg who headed a restoration of the Shroud conducted in 2002, the selvage displays an unusual double thread pattern that is also found at Masada and is associated with the Essenes.

Dr. Gilbert Raes, examining the cloth under a microscope, identified fragments of cotton fibers adhering to the Shroud that were determined to be *Gossypium herbaceum,* commonly known as Levant cotton, a variety that was in use in the Middle East as long ago as 700 B.C. and was not known to grow in Europe in the Middle Ages. It would have come onto the Shroud, which is linen, coincidentally, probably during storage. Its presence suggests very strongly that the Shroud was in the Middle East.

The image of the Man of the Shroud also suggests an origin in Roman times. First, there are around a hundred wounds caused by the distinctive dumbbell –shaped lead or bone tips called *plumbatae* that were fixed into the leather thongs of the Roman *flagrum.* The postmortem wound in the flank of the victim matches the injury that would be caused by a Roman *lancea,* a short spear with a leaf-shaped point. There are contusions along the back and shoulders that correspond with injuries that would have been caused by carrying a *patibulum.* Three of the four canonical gospels say that Simon of Cyrene was made to carry Jesus's *patibulum,* but the fourth, John, says that he carried his own cross. In either case, there are marks on the image that show that the victim fell a number of times without being able to break his fall. It seems likely that he was weakening as he struggled under the heavy crossbeam, and Simon was brought in to relieve him of its weight so that he would not die before being crucified. The victim also had a cap of thorns pressed down onto his head, not a circular crown as is portrayed in later art. In fact, there is not a single painting of the passion that shows a cap of thorns such as would have been used in the Middle East, but only a wreath, which was the style of a crown in the Western Roman Empire. The Man of the Shroud also took a facial beating, attested by his swollen and disfigured nose, the swelling around his eyes and the bruises on his face. Limestone dust recovered from the Shroud found by Dr. Riccardo Levi-Setti of the University of Chicago using a scanning electron microscope matches the limestone present in other tombs that are in the same limestone formation where the Holy Sepulcher and the Garden Tomb are located. The limestone of these tombs and the dust on the Shroud consists of calcium aragonite rather than the calcium carbonite of the more common form of limestone.

The pollens found on the Shroud have also been identified by Dr. Max Frei, a botanist and expert in Mediterranean flora. Samples were taken from the Shroud using tape that had been specially prepared so that it would only lift surface material and would not affect the cloth. He identified 58 different pollens that were present on the cloth and then spent nine years, until his death, obtaining pollen samples from the Middle East and comparing them to the Shroud samples.

He found 16 pollens from plants that are only found in deserts, 7 that grow in rocky areas, including Palestine, and 6 from Turkey and the eastern Mediterranean. While there were also pollens from plants that grow in Italy and France, none of the 29 samples mentioned above grow in either location. The pollens reveal that the Shroud was in Palestine, Anatolia, the region around Constantinople, and France and Italy. The traditional story is that it was moved to Edessa in Turkey, then to Constantinople, then back to Edessa, only arriving in France much later.

The reasons that it may have been taken from Palestine in the first place are two, both having to do with Jewish law. First, if it then contained a visible image, it could have been considered blasphemous. Second, also under Jewish law, a burial cloth was deemed unclean. Had one been found to have been removed from a tomb, the authorities might well have destroyed it.

Edessa would have been chosen as a place of safekeeping both because it lay outside of the Roman Empire at that time, and therefore also outside of the influence of both Roman and Jewish law, and because its king, Abgar, was known to be interested in Jesus and his teaching. Legend has it that there was even correspondence between the two, and that Jesus sent a disciple to Abgar, who cured an illness that he was suffering.

It is not until the sixth century that there is any mention of an image on the Shroud, which was at that time folded and apparently framed in such a way that only the face was visible. While the blast of radiation that created the image was instantaneous, it would have become visible only slowly due to the different speeds at which fibers impacted by different energy intensities were aging. The irradiated fibers would age more quickly than those the radiation had not touched. If so, then it was taken out of Judea only because of the danger of it being destroyed for being a burial garment, not for the presence of an image.

There is evidence that the Shroud, still in a folded state but by now showing a relatively clear negative image of the face, was owned during the twelfth century by the legendary

Knights Templar. When, due the fact that the French king coveted their great wealth, they were falling into disfavor in the early thirteenth century, they were rumored to worship something "like an old piece of skin, as though embalmed and like polished cloth" that was "pale and discolored." (This quote is from *The Chronicles of Saint Denis,* as quoted in Ian Wilson's *The Shroud of Turin.)*

The Shroud first emerges in France in the possession of a man called Geoffrey de Charny. When the Templars were destroyed as an institution, the two Grand Masters were burned at the stake. They were Jacques de Molay and Geoffrey de Charnay. Was this man related to Geoffrey de Charny, and was that why the Shroud was in his possession?

We will never know the answer to that question, nor exactly why the Shroud took the route that it did, but the pollens present on its surface do suggest that it was in Jerusalem, Edessa, Constantinople, France and Italy, not that it was only ever in France and Italy.

The image not only corresponds vertically to the parts of the body that were lying immediately beneath the cloth, but also with the distances of those body parts from the cloth. Thus the body had to be under the cloth when the frontal image was recorded.

That the image was formed by radiation of some kind is suggested by the colors in the linen fibers on which it appears. The linen, as a form of cellulose, has dehydrated and oxidized. While the unmarked areas of the cloth have oxidized naturally over time, something that happened to the areas of the cloth containing the image has caused them to oxidize differently, and in a very unusual way. Cellulose is made up of carbon, oxygen, and hydrogen atoms that are bonded together in pairs —that is to say, single-bonded. Whatever created the Shroud image caused breakages among these bonds. The result was that the carbon and oxygen atoms then double-bonded with each other. These trillions of double-bonded atoms are what cause the dark tan color of the image. There is little to explain such an effect except energy of some sort being emitted from the body. If this happened, the result would be a negative image, as the radiant energy that reached the cloth from the body darkened the fibers it touched more than those around them.

Only a photograph of it, as Secundo Pia accidentally discovered when taking the first Shroud photos in 1898, would produce a positive image.

The return of Jesus has long been predicted, coming in glory. But a careful reading of Revelation reveals another possibility. In Revelation 3:3, he says, "But if you do not wake up, I will come like a thief, and you will not know at what time I will come to you." Revelation is a complex document, in part a jeremiad against Rome, in part a gematria that reveals the dimensions of the New Jerusalem, and in part a mystical text that refers to the ancient idea of balance contained in the Sphinx (Rev. 4:7, "The first creature was like a lion, the second like an ox, the third had a face like a man, the fourth was like a flying eagle"). It warns about the danger of ignoring the search for inner goodness. It demands that we wake up to our own truth. Finally, it predicts that the world will end in fire, and when that happens, souls will have to face themselves as they are, for the end of the age stops change and thus ends free will.

The Jesus of Revelation slips back into the world. He does not come in glory. The reason for this is simple: if he came in glory we would see for certain the need for goodness. We could no longer choose to go in evil ways. So if something like that ever happens—the appearance of an irrefutable divine presence that we feel compelled to believe as a final authority—then the reason for our lives will also end, and there will be nothing left except for us to be judged, as Revelations would have it, or weighed against a feather upon the scales of Osiris as the Egyptians believed.

One has to wonder if his return "like a thief" took place in 1898, in the moment that Secundo Pia exposed his first photographic plate.

The blood marks on the Shroud present at least as perplexing a puzzle as the body images. Some of them could have been painted onto the cloth, but if that had happened they would have had a pattern of discoloration left by the coagulation process. There is none present. Still, even though anticoagulants were not discovered until the eighteenth century, it's possible that something was known in the past that has been lost to the record. Oddly, some of them appear to be marks that were on parts of the body that wouldn't have touched the Shroud, and they don't appear to have dripped onto it. It is hard to imagine what caused this, unless the body actually went through the Shroud cloth and the blood marks were left behind in the process.

Another oddity is the condition of the blood marks. Because blood gets darker and darker over time when exposed to air, they should be black by now. They are, however, red. The fact that they are not all drippings and that they are red was what initially convinced skeptics that they must be paint. But, after more than a dozen tests, it has been shown that they consist of human blood. How can it be, then, that after two millennia, they are still red? Even if they were added as recently as a hundred years ago, they would be dark brown by now.

There is really only one possible answer, and that is that something happened that caused some of them to transfer from the body to the cloth and also forestalled normal decomposition in all of them. Once again, radiation of some sort is one of the few things that could have caused the redness to persist and not left the residue of some sort of chemical preservative behind. So the strangely preserved state of the blood can be added to the evidence of radiation that the image suggests. When Dr. Carlo Goldoni experimented with irradiating blood with neutrons, then exposing it to light, he found that it remained red over time. So it seems possible that the radiation that affected the Shroud was composed of neutrons.

As to why some of the marks appear to have transferred from the body to the cloth instead of dripped onto it—that is not explicable unless the body, in some semi-material form, moved through the cloth, and as it did so left the blood behind on its surface.

When examined under ultraviolet light, the Shroud linen fluoresces, which would be expected. Oddly, though, like the scorches from its sixteenth century exposure to fire, the discolorations that produce the body image do not. In fact, a piece of linen can be made to scorch by heating, obviously, and an image can be produced that is somewhat like the Shroud image, but it lacks both the detail and the Shroud's unique 3D effect. Also, on the Shroud, there are no signs of pyrolytic changes in the fibers whose darkening produces the image, meaning that the scorch is not due to thermal heating. The only other possibilities are a chemical reaction and radiation, and the evidence of the use of chemicals would be plain to see under even a moderately powered microscope. There are none.

The agent that produced the image acted with decreasing intensity depending on the distance between its source and the cloth that it touched. As I have said, there is nothing to explain this except a radiation emission that came out of the body.

But if so, what kind was it and what had to have happened to release it?

Physical objects, including us, are made up of atoms which contain varying amounts of protons and neutrons. There are other particles in most atoms, but these two make up the overwhelming mass of every atom. Differing numbers of protons and neutrons are what produce variance in the nature of the physical world. The lightest element, hydrogen, contains one proton and one neutron. Much denser gold contains 79 protons and 118 neutrons. Water, which makes up 60 percent of a normal human body, contains 10 protons and 8 neutrons. Carbon, hydrogen, nitrogen and oxygen make up 99 percent of the atoms in a body. The total number of atoms in a hundred and fifty pound man is approximately 7×10^{27}—or, to put it another way, a lot.

If a body were to release particles from its atoms in the form of radiation, most of them would be protons and neutrons. While deuterium, electrons, alpha particles, and possibly some gamma rays and other radiant energies would also be emitted, protons and neutrons would be so vastly in the majority that it is to the effects that these particles might have on linen that we must look to determine if they did indeed radiate from the body of Jesus and form the Shroud image.

Protons are light and non-penetrating, so they would only have affected the outermost surface of the cellulose molecules that make up the linen fibers. Neutron radiation is very penetrating, so it would have affected the entire depth of the cloth as well as the blood and anything else present.

The straw color seen only in the top layer of molecules of the fibers would have been caused by protons. This effect was first seen in an experiment that irradiated cellulose fibers at the Harwell nuclear reactor in the UK in 1950. The nuclear age and the cold war were just beginning, and extensive testing of the effects of ionizing radiation was being done on thousands of different materials in reactors worldwide. The experiment was carried out by Dr. Kitty Little of the British Atomic Energy Research Establishment, who commented on the Shroud in a paper published in 1997 entitled "The Formation of the Shroud's Body Image."

Dr. Jean-Baptiste Rinaudo of the Center for Nuclear Medicine Research in Montpellier, France irradiated linen with protons, and found that, after radiation, the linen—which fluoresces in its natural state—no longer did so. This is exactly what is seen on the Shroud image.

Irradiation with neutrons causes something called neutron conversion in anything exposed to it. What happens is that new carbon-14 atoms will be created within irradiated material. If the Shroud was irradiated with neutrons, therefore, that would be another reason that the carbon date was advanced. The neutron radiation would have made the Shroud appear younger than it was because it would have left behind more C^{14} than would have been present if it was 2,000 years old. Dr. Goldoni's findings suggest the presence of neutron radiation, so we have both forms being emitted into the Shroud.

As Mark Antonacci points out in *Test the Shroud*, atomic and molecular testing could shed a great deal more light on what happened to it. The actual age of the Shroud could finally be determined. The precise sequence of events that resulted in the creation of the image could be determined. As Antonacci puts it, "As human beings, we have the most inherent right to all of this new and sophisticated evidence."

There is much more to be learned about the Shroud than what has been found from the tests that have been conducted since the 1988 carbon dating mistake. There is no real question that it is an entirely anomalous object—in fact, probably the strangest thing on earth.

Some sort of neutron flux, accompanied by a burst of protons, was responsible for the creation of the Shroud image. That is clear enough.

But then, incredibly, after the energy emission took place, a man who had been dead was seen to be walking around alive.

More testing can quantify the radiation emission and fix the age of the Shroud with certainty. But nothing can explain how it could be that a burst of neutrons bouncing around in a limestone tomb until their energy was expended could result in a corpse coming back to life, let alone apparently dematerializing while inside the cloth in which it was wrapped and then becoming re-animated.

Based on what is now known about the Shroud, it is obviously a mistake to dismiss the strange story of the resurrection as myth and hyperbole. At the same time, as we shall see, there is every reason to be careful with the religious doctrine that gradually emerged over the 300 years after that event.

We cannot know how, or even if, the burst of energy in the tomb led to Jesus's reappearance. It's an obvious assumption, though. Not at all obvious is what the Jesus that people saw after the resurrection event *was*. Was he once again a flesh and blood human being? If so why could he disappear and reappear the way he did, travel instantaneously to Galilee and later strike Paul with light so bright that it blinded him for days?

I would not think that the current scientific model of reality is going to be able to arrive at an explanation for the resurrected Jesus. How do we go from an unexplained burst of energy to a reanimated dead man? There is scientific evidence for the burst of energy in the tomb. There is none for the reappearance of Jesus—which is not to say that it didn't happen. On the contrary, I think, at this point, that it is safe to assume that it did. How, though—that must remain a mystery.

Despite the apparent truth and mystery of the resurrection, it doesn't follow that the doctrine of the church as we now understand it is a precise reflection of what Jesus taught. As we shall see, it is in many respects quite different, and its application has been, to say the least, uneven.

The resurrection is among the most unusual events in history, if not the most unusual. Not only the condition of the Shroud suggests that it happened, but also the reports of what Jesus did after he emerged from the tomb.

There are two levels of human relationship with higher being. In one, we have free will. In the other, we do not. This is a profoundly important line. On one side of it, choice continues to be available to us because we are in a state of unsureness. We have free will. On the other, we are certain of a divine presence and no longer able to deny its truth. Free will has ended.

It seems to me, based on Jesus's actions after he reappeared, that he knew and understood this, but I do not see any way to show that the gospel writers could have understood it. They report what is clearly a carefully orchestrated plan that was designed to inspire his followers without compromising the free will of anybody who was still on the journey of choice.

Let's see how this plan unfolded.

Matthew 28 may record the moment of resurrection. "After the Sabbath, at dawn on the first day of the week, Mary Magdalene and the other Mary went to look at the tomb. There was a violent earthquake, for an angel of the Lord came down from heaven and, going to the tomb, rolled back the stone and sat on it. His appearance was like lightning and his clothes were white as snow." (Matt. 28:1—3) The burst of energy that took place in the tomb was significant enough to cause the light that the women saw, and the shaking of the ground. In fact, this would appear to be the moment of resurrection, and the man who appeared was, if not one of his mysterious helpers, then Jesus himself.

A couple of verses later, Jesus appears to the women and makes a telling remark. He says, "Do not be afraid. Go and tell my brothers to go to Galilee; there they will see me." (Matt. 28:10)

If he was now an invulnerable magical being, why not appear in Jerusalem and thumb his nose at the authorities? A few days before, he was a popular revolutionary leader. Now here he is, in a state that is provably miraculous, so why not fulfill the ambition that brought him to Jerusalem in the first place and create an uprising? Seeing him returned from the dead, the public would have reacted exactly as did those few who saw him: they would have become fanatical followers. Instead of embarking on the torturous journey that his mission took and continues to take, he could have ascended to the throne of heaven right there and then.

I doubt that he was vulnerable at that point. But we certainly were. If he had made a general public appearance, shining with light as he did, for example, during the transfiguration, or disappearing before the eyes of witnesses, as also happened, people would have assumed that he was a living god and his every word would have become law. The whole Roman Empire, and eventually the world, would have reformed itself around his teaching—which, as Thomas so eloquently demonstrates, was exactly what he did *not* want.

The mission of Jesus was not to end our free will with a display of overwhelming authority, but to encourage us to use his teaching to find a path within ourselves that leads to a personal discovery of the realm of peace within us. As he did not reveal himself to the world transfigured, it would seem that he wished to leave the path open for us to use his teaching to seek on our own toward a new understanding of ourselves and the journey of life.

If he had been even a bit more public than he was—say, briefly walked the streets of Jerusalem—the Romans would have rounded up every friend and ally of his that they knew about, and tortured them all in a quest for information, likely executing most if not all of them. Jesus's mission would have failed in another way.

He had to leave Judea at once, both because he was not there to become an overwhelming spiritual authority, and because he did not want to appear in such a way that it led the Romans to massacre his disciples. So there's no mystery to what he did. This is also why the claim in the apocrypha that he was seen 500 days after his resurrection is probably false. He would have remained here only as long as necessary to make certain that enough people encountered him to guarantee that his message would be taken out into the whole of the world.

The ones who were destined to carry his message did have their free will compromised. "After six days Jesus took Peter, James and John with him and led them up a high mountain, where they were all alone." (He was being very careful. He knew exactly what he was doing.) "There he was transfigured before them. His clothes became dazzling white, whiter than anyone in the world could ever bleach them." (Mark 9: 2—4)

In that moment, their free will ended. They became unable to act against the will of whatever it was they were seeing, which they understood as Jesus. They had gone as far as they were going to go in terms of inner transformation. This is why they could be chosen for an experience that would end their free will. They were meant to be inspired to take his message into the world, which is precisely what they did.

As they and others tried to make sense of this completely impossible event, the Jesus movement was thrown into confusion. As I have said, the Greek and Hellenized authors of the gospels and the Acts and the letters attempted to make sense of the story by telling it both as the story of a gentile solar deity and the Jewish messiah.

Given the state of knowledge at the time, the fact that the witnesses and the gospel writers connected his story to those of the solar deities is understandable, as well as their attempt to graft it onto Jewish tradition and to connect it to the sacred number twelve, which they did because they saw it as a direct product of the mind of God. It is out of this effort, guided by a volatile combination of fanatical intensity and limited knowledge, that the doctrinal stories that are now known as Christian literalism emerged.

Who he really was, we shall not know until and unless his glorious reappearance takes place. As that will end free will it can only happen at the conclusion of the human experience on Earth.

The way he was inside, what he knew of himself, must be, until such a time, hidden from us. But one thing is no longer hidden: Thanks to the indefatigable efforts, often under very oppressive circumstances, of the community of sindinologists, or Shroud researchers, we have reason to think that an unexplained burst of radiant energy really was emitted from Jesus's corpse, and somehow continued his presence on earth for a time after his death.

The light that flashed out of his dead and rotting body was so intense that it might as well have been a spark from the sun. As it brought forth a restored version of him that walked in the world, we might also think of it as something that emerged out of an unknown science or a higher consciousness, or God, or what in Mary is called "the Good."

If the work of the Jesus Seminar is correct and the Q gospel does represent the extent of his actual teaching, then the core of it is the Beatitudes. So the path was open. It was there to be followed. Inevitably, though, the people who had been exposed to his resurrected presence were inspired to spread word of the miracle and proclaim his divinity, not so much transmit his teaching. They also brought the urgency of his prophecy that the end times—and his return in glory—were imminent.

He was wrong about the end times, but not entirely. The world that he knew did indeed end. The Roman Empire that Jesus lived in was completely destroyed.

For thirty or so years after his departure, his story was transmitted orally. As it spread, it also grew. More miracles were piled on. By the time John comes along, it has morphed into something very like one of the polytheistic cults, complete with its own mysteries and hidden codes.

Through the years that followed, there are more distortions and then still more, until it emerges, during the collapse of the empire, as state institution and a nightmarish force that turns its members into fanatical monsters. It was not the teaching that did that, though. It was the times.

How that transformation occurred is an important and terrible story, one that involves an exploration of the subtlety and dreadful power of evil, and the way it works both inside us and at the same time in the world. It is also among the most instructive stories that history offers, for understanding it can restore our access to the lost path of this great teacher. . .which is not really lost at all, as we shall see.

It is to this story that we will now turn.

13

JESUS AND THE FALL OF ROME

As is happening now on a larger scale and in a somewhat different way, around the year 150 A.D. the Roman world began to experience climate change. Their situation was different, in that it involved changes in the sun rather than an accumulation of heat-retaining gasses in the atmosphere, which is what is happening now. Over the 350 years from around 200 B.C. until the 150s A.D., the Roman world had enjoyed what is known as the Roman Climate Optimum, a long period of mild weather and generous rainfall in the Mediterranean Basin. Now, driven by reduced heat from the sun, changes in the North Atlantic Oscillation, or NAO, which is a fluctuation in air pressure over the North Atlantic, were starting to take place.

From about 200 B.C., solar output had been high and stable. This meant that temperatures were generally warm. We know this not only because of contemporary descriptions of harvests and floods and tree ring analysis, but also because stalagmites in parts of the Northern Hemisphere are sensitive to the different states of the NAO. Fluctuations in it have left a record in caves in Scotland, where the annual growth rate of the stalagmites reveals how the oscillation was performing season to season. This record goes back 3000 years.

When air pressure changes over the North Atlantic are more extreme, powerful storms result and northern Europe gets substantial rainfall. When the pressure differences are slight, storm tracks move farther south, over the Mediterranean basin. Until the mid—100s A. D., these differentials had been slight and the Mediterranean region had experienced regular seasonal rainfalls, favoring an agricultural society like the Roman Empire.

Around 150 solar output began slowly decreasing, causing the Mediterranean climate to become gradually cooler and drier. Because the empire's main grain-producing areas were concentrated along the southern shore of the Mediterranean where rainfall was always unsure, serious problems with food supply began to emerge. For the next few hundred years, this situation would grow worse and worse and worse.

Driven by years of good harvests and a stable food supply, the population of the empire had been growing since the Roman Climate Optimum established itself. The Roman peace had sped up that growth, and by 150 A.D., there were approximately 75 million people living in the Roman Empire. While most of them lived in rural areas, Rome itself had around a million inhabitants. The city had long outgrown the Servian Walls, built during its early days as a kingdom, and it was now one of the few unwalled cities in the ancient world. A fourth century A.D. census called the *Notitia* lists 46,602 apartments, 1,790 mansions and 28 libraries. In 150, the numbers were probably not that different. While in 150 a million people lived in Rome, after 500 years of continuing climate deterioration, plague and depopulation and the invasions that accompanied them, by the seventh century this grandest of all cities had been reduced to a ruin populated by perhaps 20,000 subsistence farmers.

In 150, Christianity was a little-known sect in an empire filled with little known sects. The gospels had all been written, including in all probability Mary and Thomas, and Christian communities were practicing discreetly throughout the empire, ever wary that they might come under suspicion due to the fact that their practices were believed by many, as authors like Pliny and Suetonius attest, to be bizarre and dangerous.

In reality, these little communities were probably among the strongest social groups in the empire, and among the strongest and most durable social institutions ever devised. The world is to this day filled with Christian churches and organizations of all kinds, all of them originating, in one way or another, with those early communities.

In Pliny's letter to Trajan, he reports that the Christians who had been brought before him told him that they would "meet before daybreak and sing a hymn to Christ as if he was a god." He continues "Their oath was to abstain from theft, robbery, adultery, and from breach of faith, and not to deny trust money placed in their keeping when called upon to deliver it."

This is a description of a community very much living not for themselves alone, but on behalf of one another and all whom they found to be in need. Mutual support structures, especially when they are motivated by morals as well as economics, have great durability.

As to communion, they were obviously careful to describe the ritual to him not in terms of its spiritual meaning but only in terms of what physically happened. "It had been their custom to depart and meet again to take food," he reports, "but it was of no special character and quite harmless."

As confused rumors about communion had caused suspicion among many that Christians were cannibals and blood drinkers, it is easy to understand why Pliny heard nothing of the fact that the "quite harmless" food was considered the body and blood of Jesus.

Which parts of the Christian ritual came from Jesus and which were added later has been the subject of speculation for a very long time. If Jesus was intentionally enacting the scapegoat ritual, then the Last Supper is probably accurately described in the gospels.

Christianity did not start with Jesus, but rather with Paul. It was therefore initiated by a mysterious incident involving what appears to have been Jesus in a transformed state of what can be called conscious light.

Amazingly, as we shall see, this is not the only such incident. In fact, such events have been affecting our spiritual journey for thousands of years and are, in the west at least, the single most important influence on our religious development and in many ways, our entire culture.

As we prepare to explore the fall of Rome and with it the emergence of Christianity, it's worth taking a closer look at Paul's conversion, which, as it is where Christianity started, is among the most important events in Western history.

Saul of Tarsus, a Hellenized Jew and a supporter of Rome, had recently been responsible for the murder of Saint Stephen, who ranks as the first Christian martyr.

Sometime around 34 A.D., perhaps a year or two after Jesus's crucifixion, Saul is walking to Damascus. As he approaches the city walls, he experiences a flash of light so intense that he is blinded. In Acts 9:3—7, Jesus then tells him to "go into the city where you will be told what you must do."

Saul is then led by the men traveling with him into Damascus where a "the Lord in a vision" commands a disciple named Ananias to go to him and restore his vision, which he does. (Acts 9:10—11) Ananias warns the disincarnate Jesus that Saul has persecuted his followers in Jerusalem and was on his way to Damascus to arrest "all who call on your name." (Acts 9:13)

Saul "got up and was baptized and after taking some food,

he regained his strength." (Acts 9:18—19) The restoration of his vision, of course, has two meanings. On the one hand, if the burst of light took place, then it was physical. Additionally, he was transformed from a persecutor of Jesus's followers into a disciple of the great teacher. But by whom? Was it only Ananias who instructed him? If so, he may well have been one of the group who had been assisting Jesus through the passion from the beginning.

An anonymous woman begins the process of the passion, a young man runs away naked in the night from Gethsemane, another appears in a white robe at the door of Jesus's empty tomb, and now unidentified teachers enable Saul—now Paul— to build an entire theological edifice of the utmost sophistication on the foundation of a flash of light and a voice from the beyond. Was Ananias one of them? We have no way to tell.

This mysterious group, who supported Jesus, guided him through the passion, oversaw the resurrection, and transformed Paul is the most influential single group of people in Western history—and to this day they remain so hidden that they are the subjects of little academic speculation, and only barely present in the gospel record.

Hundreds of years after Paul's death, as disaster after disaster caused the Romans to cease to believe in the power of their ancient gods, the empire would seek to link itself to the power of the deity Paul had created. This deity, Christ, was given his authority by the stories of Jesus the wonder-worker and his divinity by the story of Jesus the risen dead man.

The process of the Christianization of the empire was expanded dramatically by the emperor Constantine, starting in 324 A.D. The new god that emerged out of his efforts had only a limited amount to do with the Jesus who had lived and taught in Galilee in the early years of the first century. That Jesus was a challenging teacher with a stirring message of compassion. This new Roman Christ retained the compassion, but as a rigid

rule rather than as part of the journey toward self understanding taught in the parables and the Thomas and Mary
gospels.

Christ was a demanding deity who was very much a reflection of the Roman understanding of what gods were and what
they wanted. Christ was Sol Invictus, he was Dionysus, he was
Mithra, no longer a teacher who was there to draw wisdom out
of his followers, but a god to be worshiped.

This impulse, though, should not be dismissed as pointless.
Prayer can be powerful as a means of linking a person to a
sense of higher being and purpose, and love that seems
sublime. But it cannot generally do what the Romans expected
of sacrifice and magic, which was cure sickness, alter nature
and divert the tides of history.

From the emperor to the lowliest slave, the entire population of that empire believed that gods were responsible for the
welfare not only of the state, but also every individual life. They
had no idea even what climate was. For them, the way to
control nature was through sacrifice to their gods, and on a
scale that would cause even wealthy people to feel the pinch of
it, and the poor to be unable to fulfill the requirements at all.

As solar energy declined, drought began to spread across
the vast Central Asian steppe, which was inhabited by a population of Asiatic horsemen. These people, whom the Western
world would come to know as the Huns, began migrating west-
ward into the lands of the Magyars, or Hungarians. They, in
turn, threatened the Germanic tribes who lived pressed up
against the Danube. Across it spread the easternmost reaches
of the Roman Empire, protected behind an elaborate system of
fortifications.

By the time Constantine was occupying the imperial
throne, the Roman Empire was already under tremendous
pressure.

The trouble had started over a hundred years before,

midway through the period of Roman history identified as the era of the five good emperors. Edward Gibbon, author of *The Decline and Fall of the Roman Empire*, characterized the age in this way: "If a man were called upon to fix the period in the history of the world during which the condition of the human race was most happy and prosperous, he would, without hesitation, name that which elapsed from the death of Domitian to the accession of Commodus." This was the period between 98 and 180 A.D.

It was also the time that the Germans, pressed by the Magyars who were being pressed by the Huns, first began making serious efforts to cross into Roman controlled territory.

At the same time, the ever-expanding system of roads and the general increase in movement caused more and more population flux. People who had never before left the immediate location of their birth were now traveling long distances by road and aboard ship, and were carrying with them diseases that had always previously been localized.

Right in the middle of Gibbon's golden age, the first great pandemic of recorded history broke out.

As it happened, the medical pioneer Galen was present in Rome when the disease struck, and described its symptoms and effects clearly enough that we know that it was almost certainly smallpox. At that time, nobody in the Roman Empire had immunity. They also had no idea of germ theory and only a vague understanding of contagion. They had no soap and no effective hand-washing convention. They had no idea what was causing the illness.

Only a few Romans thought of disease the way Galen did, as some sort of a disruption of the body. Most considered that the horrific destruction that began unfolding around them was a punishment from Apollo, a solar deity who, like the others, was also a god of fertility and health. His son, Asclepius, was the patron of healing. To this day the symbol of

Asclepius, the caduceus, is the universal symbol of the medical profession.

As the plague spread, people flocked to Apollo's temples to beg forgiveness and hopefully be cured.

They were not cured.

Known as the Antonine Plague, the pandemic probably took the lives of 10 percent of the population of the empire. It caused a generalized disruption of the economy and a fiscal crisis. To maintain the army, which was urgently needed along the Danube, emperor Marcus Aurelius was forced to auction off treasures from the imperial palace in Rome. The sudden deaths of so many slaves, workers and managers caused the collapse of supply systems, with the result that famine spread across wide areas of the empire. As starvation weakens the immune system, these disruptions caused the plague to become even more virulent.

The empire was no longer based on plunder, as it had been during Jesus's time. In fact, the Judean revolt and the cost of controlling it had been one of the factors that had brought about tax reform. Still, though, people began to resist their taxes, and unrest among the German tribes across the Danube frontier encouraged Rome's traditional enemy, Parthia, to try to take advantage. Legions now had to be moved from the Danube to the east. (Parthia was roughly where Iran is now.) The plague, spreading fast, infected the army while it was in its winter quarters. Marcus's co-emperor, Lucian, died of it.

Invading barbarians penetrated into the empire, crossing the Alps and also entering the Balkans. During these tumultuous times, Marcus, who was a truly remarkable and capable man, also completed one of the great works of philosophical literature, his *Meditations*, which chiefly concern detachment from the trials and desires of life and pursuit of an objective hauntingly familiar from the Mary gospel, which he, also, called "the good."

The Christian community was still small and persecutions were relatively rare, but there is mention in the writings of Eusebius of one at Lyon in 177. The way Eusebius describes it, it was apparently a local affair brought about by the suspicion that the Christians' failure to sacrifice to the gods was causing the plague. There is no evidence that Marcus himself engaged in any persecutions, but the theme that those who denied the gods their sacrifices would bring down their wrath on all was clearly present in the popular imagination.

In that time, the Christians were living in much the same way as they had in the years immediately after the disciples' missionary activities began.

Their community, with its emphasis on cooperative living and the support of all for one, would have been more resilient to the disruptions caused by the plague than the less-organized society at large.

The Antonine Plague did not cause the Romans to lose faith in their gods, and after it ended, the empire recovered. However, as yet more ships and roads were built and personal mobility increased, there was more movement than ever. The continuing pressure on the border from the outside also drove many vulnerable farmers and rural workers deeper into the interior.

This all meant ever more exposure to new diseases, and local epidemics became more and more common.

Then, a hundred years after the Antonine plague had sputtered out, there emerged an even worse one, which history calls the Plague of Cyprian. Unfortunately, with Galen now long dead and nobody to replace him, there is no description of its symptoms definite enough to enable us to do more than guess what caused it. What is clear is that it was devastating, far more so than the Antonine Plague. It started in 249 and lasted, in its first phase, for around fifteen years, with an apparent recurrence around 270 A.D., twenty-one years later.

We know of its effects from a sermon given by Cyprian, the bishop of Carthage. He describes eye pain, fever, generalized malaise, uncontrollable diarrhea, throat lesions, vomiting, the destruction of the limbs of some people, and blindness. Its onset was abrupt and its course swift. Cyprian says that it raced through the population "like a fire." The illness was accompanied by a thirst so great that, as Cyprian describes it, "The springs and streams and cisterns were full of those burning with thirst." One account suggests that the population of Alexandria declined by something like 60 percent. In Athens and Rome, 5,000 a day were said to be dying.

The disease may have been, like the Antonine Plague, smallpox, but as there is no description of the characteristic rash, it might also have been a particularly virulent influenza or even something like Ebola.

During the decade preceding the onset of the illness, climate disturbance had increased steadily, with floods and droughts and consequent disruptions in food distribution. Thus, when the disease appeared, a significant part of the empire's population was probably malnourished and so more than usually vulnerable.

It was during this plague that the Christian community began to grow to the point that it became a noticeable part of the social fabric of the empire. The Christian community helped each other, the healthy protecting the children of the sick, those with food reaching out to those with none. They did not discriminate against anybody. If you went to them for help, they did what they could. During the later Plague of Justinian, men would be organized into a minor clerical order called the *parabalini*, or risk takers. They would carry the sick to hospitals and the dead to graveyards, ignoring the danger to themselves.

As conditions in the empire worsened, they would evolve from a group of brave helpers into fanatical terrorists who would be responsible for the murder of the great astronomer and philosopher Hypatia, who was torn apart by a crazed mob in Alexandria in 415 A.D. By that time, many Romans had come to believe that the old gods weren't just indifferent, but were actually the cause of the empire's troubles, and sought to eradicate them completely. Thus a pagan like Hypatia came to be regarded as an enemy of the human community itself, and visiting a horrible death upon her was thought to lessen the power of her gods and please Christ.

That would all come later, though. In 250, Rome did not care one way or another about a community with its own parallel organization that was not controlled by the state, but it did want to be certain that everybody was participating in the state religious cult. The gods were not cooperating with mankind, and the reason was thought to be a general decline in worship. The emperor Decius decreed that everyone in the empire would be required to engage in an act of sacrifice. Coins began to be minted appealing to "Apollo Salutaris" (Apollo the Healer). People had not only to sacrifice, but also to obtain a certificate from a magistrate confirming that they had done so. The edict involved has not survived, but some of the certificates have, and they appear to require sacrifice to the emperor as divine, not to the Roman pantheon in general.

Many Christians, of course, would not sacrifice at all, let alone to the emperor. They therefore suffered the ultimate penalty. The victims included Fabian, the bishop of Rome. Christian communal property such as churches and meeting houses was also confiscated.

This did not prevent the steady spread of the religion, as can be seen from the fact that, over the half century from 250 to 300, more and more Christian personal names are found on papyri in Egypt and on tombs. At the same time, temples were being let to go to seed, and state worship, despite the decree of Decius, appears to have continued its decline.

As the old gods failed them, more and more people were turning to a new one.

Because the people were losing faith in the state's gods, they were also necessarily losing faith in the state. They had all sacrificed, pouring their money and goods into the coffers of the temples, but what good had it done? They had no idea that, 93 million miles away, the fickle star upon which we are totally dependent was emitting less and less energy, which would in no way be changed by cutting the throats of animals or destroying expensive possessions, or, for that matter, by prayer.

In 200, there is little mention of Christianity. By 300, everything has changed. As the old gods continue to fail, Christianity expands faster and faster. Because of that core nature as a community, Christians think of their practice not as a cult or a mystery, but as an *ethnos*, a nation. The devotees of Apollo or Sol Invictus are loyal to their god but also willing to sacrifice to others. By its very nature, polytheism is not exclusive. The Christians were different. To them, Christ as part of the Holy Trinity *was* god, and they were his worshipers, the Christian Nation.

Decius did not single out Christians for persecution. The law stated that anybody who failed to sacrifice (except Jews, who were exempt) would suffer the penalty of death.

Despite the fact that they weren't singled out, the persecution fell most heavily on the Christians. The more they endured the combination of plague and persecution, the stronger their sense of community became. Because Jesus had said "Whenever two or three are gathered in my name, I am with them," the community was itself a thing of God, and Cyprian could write that "only two or three gathered together in unanimity. . .may obtain from the majesty of God what they ask."

This personalization of the relationship between the human and the divine through the community was a novel aspect of the Jesus movement, and now, in a time of incredible stress, it became a powerful inducement to join the community. Add to that the fact that the community was welcoming and supportive and forgiving, and it is not surprising that Eusebius, writing of the period of the plague and famine, described the actions of the Christians and the reaction to them this way: "For they alone in the midst of such ills showed their sympathy and humanity by their deeds. Every day, some continued caring for and burying the dead, for there were multitudes who had no one to care for them; others collected in one place those who were afflicted by the famine throughout the entire city, and gave bread to them all; so that the thing was spoken about by everybody, and they praised the god of the Christians. . ."

He could further state that "in every city congregations gathered and assemblies thronged. . .and every one of the unbelievers was astonished, wondering at so marvelous a transformation. . ."

More than any other event, the Plague of Cyprian established Christianity as a force in the Roman world. As it faded, it left behind a devastated and profoundly changed empire. One thing that the average person, perhaps a girl whose entire family had died and who must either prostitute herself or starve, could do was to turn to the Christians and be taken in and begin a new life in the community. Jesus had left behind a clear set of personal ethics that went beyond commandments forbidding wrongdoing. Instead, he had laid down a whole way of life that was based on the belief that every person had a value that was not connected to his status but simply to his existence.

Writing in 2 Corinthians, Paul had described how the Macedonian churches reacted to "a very severe trial," saying that "their overflowing joy and their extreme poverty welled up in rich generosity. For I testify that they gave as much as they were able, and even beyond their ability." (2 Cor. 8: 2—3). This was a model based on the example set in Beatitude 7, "Beloved are those who make peace, for they will be called children of God." (Matt. 5:7)

The Roman world of the third century was desperate in ways that we, even in our own age of plague and climate change, cannot presently imagine. There was no such thing as a social safety net. The plague was a mysterious curse sent by supernatural beings. The barbarians were ruthless murderers from which the state offered less and less protection. The fertility gods had failed to bring in harvests. Fortuna, the terrifying goddess who controlled fortune good and bad, was on an inexplicable rampage. She had taken the Romans' luck from them, as Apollo had taken their health and Ceres their food. People desperate for every scrap they could get their hands on could hardly burn it in sacrifice to indifferent or hostile gods.

The Christian community was virtually the only refuge a Roman could turn to in the terrible times of the late 200s. From all accounts, it was still innocent, in the sense that it was open to all and was tolerant of all.

Then, starting in the early 300s, history's most ferocious and life-altering revolution began. It overturned the culture and civilization of the Western world as it then existed. While it brought some very real benefits, it also irrevocably diminished the store of human knowledge in ways from which there can be no recovery.

This great tragedy began in the mind of one man, who failed to understand the most fundamental warning Jesus left behind.

And so enters Constantine.

14

THE CITIES OF THE PLAIN

Jesus's missionaries had traveled the Roman Empire spreading his basic message that everybody has equal value in the eyes of God, that we should love one another, and, above all, that we can find the realm of heaven in our own hearts.

Rome transformed the missionary spirit of those early followers into something very different. This process did not start with the official Romanization of Christianity in the fourth century, but paralleled the increasing size of the Christian population, as the bishops tried to maintain a consistency of worship—and fought among themselves with increasing bitterness over what that should be.

The lines were drawn: either Jesus was God as man, or God *in* a man. Neither side considered the idea that Jesus might be, simply, human, and that what he did might actually reflect that he was in a human state that even now we do not allow ourselves to believe is possible.

When Rome officially adopted Christianity as its state religion, the cross, which had been a symbol of human courage in the face of oppression, became a battle standard, which it would remain long after the empire fell.

Jesus as Christ thus became, like Jehovah and Zeus and Athene and so many others before him, a war god. Deuteronomy records the Israelite's conquest of Canaan, saying that they took "all the cities of the plain and all Gilead" (Deut 3:10). Like old Gilead, the Roman Empire was ruled from its cities and defined by them. While its rural population was greater, its wealth was gathered in its cities, and control of them was control of the empire.

They were filled with magnificent public buildings, graceful temples, baths, and theaters. They were watered by aqueducts and served with sewers, and provided with supplies from across the whole empire. They contained the greatest concentration of wealth mankind had ever known and were therefore the ultimate prize. The man who ruled over them was the richest and most powerful in the world, so exalted that he was called a god —as long as he managed to dominate the madcap king-of-the-mountain political process that had evolved in the absence of an established rule of succession.

It was into this beautiful, damaged and chaotic world, which had, between 250 and 284 had been ruled by fifteen different emperors, that a political genius called Flavius Valerius Constantinus came, bringing with him singular skills both as a soldier and a politician, and deep insight into the structural problems that were causing the empire to falter. Constantine was brilliant, but also flawed. And because of his flaws, he made one of history's truly great mistakes.

He did not become a Christian until he was on his deathbed, but he had more influence on Christianity than anybody except Paul and Jesus.

Constantine was the child of Flavius Valerius Constantius I and his first wife, Helena Augusta. She had risen from the peasant class after being noticed by Constantius, supposedly because the two of them were wearing identical bracelets when their paths crossed. While Eusebius says that Helena was converted to Christianity by her son, it seems possible that, coming from the lower classes as she did, she was already a Christian, and it was her influence on him that drew him toward Christianity, not the other way around. As the purpose of Eusebius's *bios* of Constantine was not to present the facts, but to use them as the basis of a heroic story about the emperor, he would have been unlikely to attribute something as important as his conversion to anybody except Jesus himself, let alone, in that age, to a woman and a peasant.

In 306, after the death of Constantius, Constantine was proclaimed emperor by the troops who were serving under him in Britain.

At that time, the empire was managed by what amounted to a committee of emperors and sub-emperors—his father had been one of the latter—so Constantine did not rule alone. When he gained the purple, the long reign of the emperor Diocletian, which lasted twenty-one years from 284 to 305, had just ended. Diocletian's co-emperor Maximan still ruled in the west, and Galerius and Constantinus were his sub-emperors. It was to his father's role that Constantine's troops had elevated him.

The reign of Diocletian had seen the only organized, empire-wide attempt to eradicate the Christian community and suppress Christian worship. Unlike the Decian persecution, which applied to anybody who refused to worship the emperor and possibly also the state gods, the Persecution of Diocletian was aimed directly at the Christians—despite the fact that his wife Prisca was one.

Like Decius before him, Diocletian was striving to save the empire by enlisting the power of the gods. When he gained the throne, the Plague of Cyprian had just recently receded and the empire was in an economic shambles and suffering from severe depopulation. As if it had lost a great war, the army was decimated.

To restore the empire, Diocletian called on the only force he knew that might be great enough, which was that of the gods.

He went to the Oracle of Apollo to find out what was wanted, and came away confirmed in the belief that, if the Christians were persecuted fiercely enough, life for the Roman people would improve.

Beginning in 303, he announced anti-Christian edicts that prohibited any and all Christian assemblies no matter where they were held, and directed that Christian churches should be razed and the sacred books of the cult burned. Unless they sacrificed to the state gods, Christian clergy were to be arrested.

It was a fierce persecution, and had it continued for very long and been consistent across the whole empire, it might have damaged the Christian movement more; but Diocletian abdicated due to ill health in 305 and on April 30, 311, Galerius, who had once encouraged him to start the persecution, now joined his co-emperors, including Constantine, in ending it.

In 311, the Edict of Serdica, also known as the Edict of Toleration, was issued by Galerius. It affirmed, for the first time in history, universal religious freedom, meaning that Christians could now worship openly. This did not mean that it was no longer necessary to respect the gods of the state, but it did mean that nobody who worshiped other gods was acting contrary to law. It also specifically returned to the Christians the churches and other property that had been confiscated under Diocletian.

The purpose of these confiscations had been to disrupt the community by depriving it of places of assembly. All Christian meetings were forbidden. The result was that the Christian community had returned to the old "house worship" system that had prevailed in its early days, carrying out its assemblies secretly.

Now, with the churches re-opened, Christians poured into them, according to Eusebius to the point that they were filled to bursting. Even during the persecution, it appears that the religion had been growing, largely due to the now well-known generosity of the Christians. While the old religion was still powerful and its adherents determined to preserve it, the more people struggled with things like sickness and economic chaos, the bigger and more organized the Christian community became.

As Christ became important in the empire, the fuzzy connection between his story and that of the sun gods rose more to the surface. Constantine explored the idea of dedicating the empire to Sol Invictus, and coinages were issued that showed his profile along with that of Sol, but in the end, he decided that the old Roman gods must be entirely replaced, and that Jesus as Christ, the living dead man, was the right choice.

In part, he did this in order to use the Christian community as the foundation for a new kind of state that would be more durable than the one organized around the old polytheism. It had arisen out of a distant agrarian past and had no social groups similar to the Christian system. Christianity was an urban movement that largely involved the poor, including slaves.

Because of stories such as the transfiguration and Paul's blinding encounter with Jesus, Christ was seen as a deity of light. As his passion fit the structure of the deaths and rebirths of other scapegoat gods, it may well have seemed to Constantine that his cult could be understood by the broad mass of people in familiar terms, as they already worshiped many solar deities.

The official reason that Constantine chose Christ over Sol

Invictus was that, during a battle with a rival called Maxentius on the Milvian Bridge in Rome on October 28, 312, he claimed to have seen the image of a cross superimposed on the disk of the sun. This symbolically connected Christ with the resplendent Sol and, because his cross was in front of the sun, specifically identified him as the more powerful of the two gods. As Constantine's defeat would have meant that the total Christianization of the empire would probably never have happened, the battle must certainly be named as among the most important ever fought in the Western world.

A year later, in 313, the Edict of Milan was decreed. It stated that "no man whatever should be refused complete toleration. . .in the practice of whatever worship he has chosen."

The edict finally freed the Christians from any chance of persecution, but did not please the Christian bishops, who saw toleration of the old polytheism as an affront to God. The average person did not share this view, and it became common practice to add Christ to the list of gods that one already worshiped. This can be seen on gravestones from the period that invoke both Christ and the gods of the underworld.

Initially, Constantine himself was not exclusively Christian. There is a coin showing him with the god Apollo and he allowed a temple to be built dedicated to himself and the imperial family as if they were, like earlier emperors, to be worshiped as divine. Instead of being declared a god, though, he had himself designated as "equal to the apostles." In other words, he was to be thought of as a thirteenth apostle, Judas Iscariot having been banished by his betrayal and suicide.

The number 13 is associated with bad luck and betrayal, and Constantine did indeed embark on as profound a betrayal as has ever been carried out: he betrayed not only civilization as it then existed, but the underlying culture, core ways of thinking and knowledge on which it rested.

The Christianity of this period had become quite different

from the Jesus path as it had been practiced during his life and in the fifty or so years following his death. To all but a few Christians of the period, Jesus was no longer the teacher of the Thomas gospel, goading his disciples into discovering their own understanding instead of looking to him for answers. Similarly, the Jesus of the Gospel of Mary was now ignored, if not already lost. In 367, Athanasius, the Bishop of Alexandria, would condemn the use of "heretical" books, which included Thomas and Mary. So thorough was the destruction of many of these books that the only copies we have ever found come from the Nag Hammadi trove.

The idea of seeking inwardly with the *nous,* the inner eye—which Jesus counsels Mary to do in that extraordinary gospel—cannot be part of a religion that seeks safety through divine favor. Such a religion is about worship of an exterior deity, not about seeking internal enlightenment.

If you are going to preserve the wealth of an empire, you need a god who cares about the material world, not the quiet inner journey toward the light. You need a god who will respond to prayers for the salvation of the cities and the armies and the emperor, not a teacher who seeks to help his followers open the door to inner peace.

The Plague of Cyprian had faded in 262, but the effects of its devastation were still being felt throughout the empire when Constantine came to power in 306. Whole regions had been depopulated by it and, judging from the relentless price inflation that continued unabated after it ended, farming and supply lines continued to be disrupted.

In a world that had experienced mass death, the promise of an afterlife was becoming more and more important. In the late 200s and early 300s, most families would have memories of loved ones lost in the plague. People wanted to believe that they were still somewhere, and wanted to be assured that there was a route to that place that they also could follow.

So not only had the old gods not been induced to help the state by its persecution of the Christians, but Graeco-Roman polytheism did not offer a clear vision of an afterlife. Instead, it told stories of a vague underworld that in some versions seemed to actually be a trap for souls. The Egyptian religion, as well as some mystery cults like the Eleusinian Mysteries, offered a route that was similar to the Christian one, but without an economic and cultural community that extended into everyday life. The older mysteries also involved complicated and costly rituals. By contrast, Christians could share in the grace of Jesus with nothing more than a crust of bread and a swallow of wine.

With their world under extreme pressure, the Romans began to ask themselves a question identical to one that we ask today, and which we will ask with more and more intensity as our own difficulties increase: How can we help ourselves? We turn to science and, to a lesser extent, religion. They had only their gods.

As the temples were being abandoned and people were flocking to non-traditional cults like Christianity, Constantine decided—as it turned out correctly—that the solution was to identify the state with a new god. Even though his cult was small, Christ, with his connection to the familiar solar deities, must have seemed an ideal choice. Because of this and also because of Constantine's deep love for his Christian mother, he decided to go beyond the Edict of Milan and further empower the Christian community.

Superficially, this would seem to be nothing more than a logical political expedient, but it had tremendous repercussions, far beyond anything anybody at the time could have imagined, for there emerged out of it both one of the greatest disasters and also one of the greatest blessings that have ever befallen mankind.

To understand this, we must explore a particular aspect of

evil as it relates to the teaching of Jesus. I refer here to a form of self-deception that causes people committing acts of evil to imagine that they are, in fact, doing good.

Just as they allowed themselves to be deceived, Constantine allowed himself to become a deceiver. Had he understood the teaching of Jesus on evil and temptation, things might not have turned out as they did.

The specific Jesus teaching I refer to here is best summarized in Matthew 4, which describes his time in the desert after completing his baptism with John. After tempting Jesus in a number of ways, Satan offers him the world if only he will change his allegiance: "The devil took him to a very high mountain and showed him all the kingdoms of the world and their splendor. 'All this I will give you,' he said, 'if you will bow down and worship me.'" (Matt. 4:8—9) Jesus refuses, and dedicates himself to God.

This has both an external political meaning and an internal spiritual meaning. It is a warning about political power, which is always in danger of becoming evil if it is not proactively directed toward the good. It is a spiritual reminder to be humble enough to recognize when one is serving one's own ambition at the expense of the needs of others.

Constantine was captured by the temptation that Jesus resisted. To save the "kingdoms of the world," that is to say, the state, he decided to look upon Christ a new version of the traditional gods, not as the teacher that he actually was, or in the context of the deeper and more true aspect of the divine that shines through his humanity.

In 324, he became sole Roman emperor. Once alone in power, he proved to be a dynamic leader, but also a tyrant. In 326, he had his second wife Fausta and his eldest son (by his first wife) Crispus murdered. Crispus was poisoned and Fausta appears to have been boiled or suffocated in an overheated bath. Crispus was murdered for plotting against him, Fausta for adultery—possibly with Crispus.

Constantine loved material things. By Roman standards, he was an incredibly elaborate dresser. At the Council of Nicea, where the fundamental beliefs that Christians would be obligated to follow were established, Eusebius describes him as moving "through the midst of the assembly like some heavenly messenger of God, clothed in a garment which glittered as though radiant with light, reflecting the glow of a purple robe, and adorned with the brilliant splendor of gold and precious stones." A messenger, yes, but perhaps not one of God's.

He had a fierce temper and, like everybody who reached the apex of power in the Roman Empire, lived in constant fear of betrayal and assassination. To survive, an emperor had to be brutal. He had to act on suspicions whether he could confirm them or not. In order that he could continue his brutality unchecked throughout his reign, Constantine did not get baptized until he was on his deathbed, believing that this subterfuge would somehow save him from damnation. He did not understand that it is real remorse, deeply explored and felt, that draws compassion, not mumbled words.

As we have seen, the decline of the old religion was already far advanced by Constantine's time. Decius had compelled the entire empire to sacrifice. Diocletian had tried to stamp out the Christians by persecution and confiscation of their meeting places. These efforts hadn't improved anything, and so people were giving up on the gods and their costly sacrificial requirements at an ever faster rate.

Due to the way the ancient world described itself, and perhaps also because of the vast destruction of texts that accompanied the Christian Revolution, we cannot determine the degree to which people related the troubles they were experiencing to an abandonment by the old gods, but it can be deduced from the horrific violence that was visited on their temples, their libraries, their priesthoods, and everything to do with them that, once unleashed, public rage against them was ferocious.

There is little evidence of what was happening during this chaotic period of plague and disruption, but according to Roger S. Bagnall in *Egypt in Late Antiquity,* the last known lists of temple personnel and property found in Egypt date from 259. This probably means that there was a general abandonment taking place across the empire, but there are no records to confirm this.

Constantine made laws that restricted idolatry—that is to say, the worship of the old gods, who were personified in the statues that stood in their temples. He also ordered the building of Christian churches, thus setting off an extraordinary architectural revolution across the entire empire. He was trying hard to please the empire's new god.

As Christian power grew, so did Christian intolerance. Over the next two centuries, the destruction of the polytheistic culture would expand until most temples were torn down, the statuary of the gods broken up or defaced, the jewels and precious metals that decorated them sold and, most tragically, the libraries burned.

After Constantine's death, with the exception of the brief reign of Julian the Apostate, the dismemberment of the old culture continued. In 341, Constantine's son, the emperor Constantius II, forbade sacrifice altogether. "Superstition shall cease and the madness of sacrifices be abolished." In 356, he made it illegal to worship images. Worship of the old gods now carried a penalty of death. In 381, Theodosius ordered the persecution of polytheists (now call pagans, or primitives) in Rome. He ended pagan festivals and orders.

This was when the *parabalani* changed from courageous hospitallers into murderous terrorists, and were implicated in the horrific murder of Hypatia in 415, which took place during the vandalism of the vast Temple of Serapis, probably the most magnificent temple then in existence.

During the early 400s, Christians destroyed most of the temples of Alexandria, pillaging not only its great temple dedicated to Serapis, but also another 2,500 other religious sites. We know this number because a fifth century city register has survived which contains records of the destruction. It is described in detail in *From Temple to Church* by Johannes Hahn, Stephen Emmel and Ulrich Gotter.

While the destruction of the Library of Alexandria is dated by Edward Gibbon in his *Decline and Fall of the Roman Empire* to 415 A.D., in fact the library declined slowly from about 150 A.D. However, the striking lack of books from the classical period can only mean that the libraries of the Roman world were generally abandoned and their contents either left to rot or actually destroyed.

New religions, when they arise, usually demonize their predecessors, and Romanized Christianity not only did this, it declared all of the works written by practitioners of the old religions to be demonic, too, thus ensuring their destruction.

The eradication of the old books was incredibly thorough, and continued for at least two hundred years, and probably much longer. The sublime excellence of what survived—from the plays of the Athenian dramatists to the works of Euclid and Plato and Aristotle, and fortunately enough else to allow us to at least gain an inkling of what must have once been—tells us that high levels of culture and science had been reached in the ancient world.

Fragmentary technological survivals such as the exquisitely machined Antikythera Device, which was found in a wreck off the Greek island of Antikythera in 1901, suggest that the technological knowledge needed to produce such things was also lost, perhaps even in the Alexandria library's branch in the temple of Serapis, still perhaps the greatest collection of scientific texts in the ancient world at that time. Reconstructions of the device have shown that it was an analog computer that was able to predict stellar and lunar movement and calculate dates for events such as the four-year Olympiads. We know of no ancient process that could have been used to manufacture its precision gearing, or who designed it, let alone the craft tradition that enabled its construction. It appears to have been built around 87 B.C., and it was not until the fourteenth century that devices of equal complexity began to be made again.

There must have been a written record of a science of predictive chronology probably at least as sophisticated as the science of geometry that has survived, but there is no trace of it left.

Somewhere between 500,000 and 700,000 scrolls may have existed in Alexandria, and undoubtedly millions more in the many smaller libraries that were present in every city in the Roman Empire. It was not only that books were lost, and the rituals of the ancient mysteries and their meanings, but an entire culture of ancient standing and enormous human validity, and perhaps even the secret of another mystery, which is what happened in Jesus's tomb.

We will never know.

The loss of the recorded intelligence of the ancient world was an unparalleled catastrophe, and given that sophisticated technology like the Antikythera Device seems to come out of nowhere, a great deal of that knowledge must have entirely disappeared.

This is due in great part to the traditional zeal of the Christian community, which was magnified after it became part of the Roman state, thus gaining the power to enforce its beliefs.

That zeal was a radical departure from the approach of the nature religions. There were no missionaries wandering the roads proclaiming the divinity of Apollo or Ceres, not like the disciples going from town to town and crying out in public spaces that Jesus was a god because he had risen from the dead.

The nature religions followed the seasons or the actions of natural objects, or reflected human psychology. Apollo, as the sun, traversed the sky every day. Ceres was the spirit of fertility that lived in the fields. Athene was the *daimon* goddess of Athens, at once the support and companion of her soldiers in battle and the source of her philosophers' wisdom. While blasphemy was possible in the old religions, of course, conversion by persuasion was not a common practice. Only when the devotees of one god overpowered those of another did conversion take place, and then generally by force. If somebody became a devotee of one of the old gods, it was usually due to some connection to the aspect of nature that the god represented. Thus Ceres did not have many worshipers in the cities, but in the countryside signs of her cult were everywhere.

The opening paragraph of the *Florida,* ("The Place of Flowers"), a collection of extracts from speeches by the first century author Apuleius, describes how a polytheistic traveler in the Roman Empire would have experienced the presence of religion on a journey: "It is a common custom with religious travelers, when they come upon some grove or sacred place, to beseech favor. . .For the traveler can find no fitter motive for a religious stop as a garlanded altar, or a shady grove sacred to some deity, or an oak decorated with horns, or a beech overspread with skins, or even a hillock consecrated to a god, or a tree trunk carved with an image, or grass wet with a libation, or a stone covered with sacrificial ointment."

Apuleius travels through a world enchanted by believers who respect as they go along the road the offerings and signs that have been left by others to indicate that one place or another is sacred, as often as not to a deity that they themselves cannot even identify. It is an accepting, passive experience of the holiness of the world.

Contrast this with the words of Jesus: "Go into all the world and preach the gospel to all creation. Whoever believes and is baptized will be saved, but whoever does not believe will be condemned." (Mark 16: 15—16) Be a missionary. Take the religion with you. Tell others. When you add to that the fact that, in the early days, some of the people who carried that message had also personally witnessed him in some way after his death, or believed this, it is not hard to understand the zeal that characterized the early Jesus movement.

The old religions arose out of the hope of controlling nature. The Jesus teaching originally had nothing to do with that. It was a path toward goodness, that is to say, toward joining oneself to the moral course of God. A desperate Roman emperor, in search of a replacement for the old, failed nature gods, distorted it in the hope that Jesus, if worshiped, would become an effective protector of the state. As Zeus and Apollo and the others in the ancient pantheon had before him, Jesus as Christ became an object of worship and supplication.

This buried the message that the path to the realm of heaven does not depend on worship but rather on an inner process of harmonizing one's own life with the Jesus teaching, most particularly the Beatitudes.

Jesus sought to save souls. Constantine sought to save the Roman Empire. Jesus resisted the temptation to accept "the kingdoms of the world" offered to him by Satan. Constantine, who was responsible for his kingdom, was in no position to resist, and dared not believe that he was only replacing old religious illusions with a new one.

While Constantine immortalized the Jesus teaching, making certain that it would never be lost to the world, he institutionalized a distortion of it that compromised its value, very nearly destroying it completely.

This supremely powerful man, swaying through the Council of Nicea in his robes and jewels, intent on preserving the lives and happiness of his subjects as well as his own, was simply not equipped to deal with the subtle truth of Jesus's message that "the realm of heaven is within you," let alone integrate difficult and contradictory writings like the Gospel of Thomas into a religion that was expected to make sense to the average Roman.

Once it was decided that worship of Christ and only Christ was what would save the state, it followed that the old gods must be demonized. Sacrificing to them hadn't helped. Very well, that was now illegal. They were not gods at all, but monsters, and the people who had sacrificed to them had been deceived by them.

It took hundreds of years of pillage of the old culture to purify the empire, and the fanatical intolerance that this involved eventually expanded into a 1400 hundred year long nightmare of injustice and murder, accompanied by the methodical suppression of knowledge and scientific endeavor. It would not formally end until the Spanish Inquisition was abolished on July 15, 1834 by Maria Christina de Borbon, Spanish Regent and Queen of the Two Sicilies, and to this day persists in a sanitized form in some of the more intolerant Christian sects.

And yet, at the same time, Christianity was as it remains to this day, a unique force for good in the world. The same religious leaders who thought nothing of burning people alive because they did not agree with accepted dogma, or simply because they were polytheists or Jews, also engaged in often very extensive acts of compassion and charity.

The oppression began with the codification of belief that took place at the first Council of Nicea. This and the seven ecumenical councils that followed over the next 400 years all dealt with shadings of the same issue: A priest called Arius maintained that Jesus was a human being especially filled by God with divine knowledge, not God in human form. In other words, he was a teacher, not a deity, but still specially connected to one.

If he was human, even though divinely connected, then there was room to interpret his words and to discover through them what a relationship with God might mean for oneself. If he was God incarnate, then his every word must be taken literally, and never mind the contradictions that fill the gospels.

If Constantine was going to be able to use the church as an arm of the state, he needed Christian doctrine to be consistent. This was for the same reason that the secular laws had to be consistent. If laws are contradictory or ambiguous, they aren't much of a foundation for government. But there was another reason: since the old gods no longer favored the empire, he wanted to induce Jesus to take their place. Therefore, he had to be sure that the worship that was being devised satisfied "the Lord."

During the period after the Edict of Milan, Christianity came into public view as a confusion of different liturgies and ideas. Constantine called all 1800 bishops together to hammer out a consistent creed and resolve once and for all the question of whether or not Jesus was a human being. It was decided that he was part of God, not a human. Arian was wrong. The creed that came out of the council spells this out with the words, "We believe in one god, the Father Almighty...and in one Lord Jesus Christ, the Son of God, begotten of the father. . .not made." Jesus and God are of the same essence. The last words of the original creed make it very clear that those who believe that he was human are anathema. "Those who say that there was a time when He was not. . .or is changeable or alterable are condemned by the holy universal and evangelical church."

Because of that word "condemned," many a fire would be lit at the feet of many a desperate human being, for many generations.

With his creed, Constantine established an orderly

approach to the new god. In doing so, he restored the willingness of the people to believe that the empire was not only a secular state, but loved and protected by higher forces. To accomplish this, he created a belief system so inflexible and a governing body so rigidly hierarchical that the church that emerged out of it has problems to this day adapting to change.

In a period when emperors often came and went over just a matter of months, Constantine's reign lasted thirty-one years. At the end of this period, the Roman Empire was once again stable, its currency was no longer in an inflationary free fall, its official institutions were functioning smoothly, and its armies were able to defend its borders.

To all appearances, the destruction of the old religion had worked. Jesus had replaced Apollo and Zeus and the other failed gods. But nature is numbers, not gods, and over the next century the numbers kept adding up less and less favorably to Rome. The effect of the pressure on food supplies can be seen in two statistics. The first is that, while there were no pandemics in the fourth and fifth centuries, malnutrition was a constant problem and with it suppressed immune systems. Fourteen regional epidemics have been identified in the fourth century and a further eighteen in the fifth. Again and again, drought would be followed by famine and then an increase in disease. The other factor, archaeologists have determined, is that the Romans of this period were getting smaller. This would have been due to generational malnutrition.

Because of the weakening of the imperial system, barbarians, driven by pressure from behind, began entering the empire. In 410, for the first time in 800 years and only the second in its history, Rome itself was sacked.

The reaction of the population to the apparent failure of Christ to protect them was startlingly different from their reaction to the failure of the old gods. The more suffering and disruption there was, the more fanatically Christian people became. Instead of resenting having to make sacrifices that were ignored, as in the past, they came to feel that their piety was inadequate.

The highly organized Christian communities held together under pressure, and the fact that Jesus was not answering prayers only drove them to more and more desperate efforts to gain his favor.

As a result, there was born a fearsome self-punishment movement. In 423, Simeon the Stylite, who had been driven out of his monastery because of his extremely austere ways, began living on top of a pole near Aleppo in Syria. His pole became a popular place of pilgrimage, and pole-sitting hermits proliferated in the Christian world.

The climate continued to fail to notice these efforts to atone for an imaginary "original sin," but its variability meant that there were long periods of stability, and by the early 400s, the empire had yet again regained much of its lost strength. Perhaps pole sitting affected nature after all, but the more certain answer is that the North Atlantic Oscillation moved in such a way that a period of regular rainfall once again visited the Mediterranean Basin.

Unfortunately, the sun soon resumed its long sleep, and drought returned. With it came famine and economic dislocation, and, this time, a huge immigration from the east, far too extensive for the imperial border guards to suppress. One German tribe after another moved into Roman territory, bringing with them their own ideas of government and moral order. Italy and Gaul were overrun. A seagoing tribe called the Vandals occupied much of North Africa.

In 476, the vestments of Romulus Augustulus, the last emperor in the west, a boy of fourteen, were loaded aboard ship and conveyed across the Mediterranean to Constantinople. Romulus was the son of Orestes, a Roman official who had for a time been the secretary of Attila the Hun. The boy, named for the founder of Rome and nicknamed for its greatest emperor, quickly disappeared into history, and with him the Roman Empire in the west. Italy became a kingdom ruled by a German tribal leader called Odoacer.

The climate continued to deteriorate. Lakes declined, rivers ran low or not at all, and famines are increasingly mentioned in the written record.

Then came the horrific year of 536, which to this day remains arguably the worst year in human memory. Over the course of the first few months of 536, the sun became less and less bright, until, by the time summer had come there was no summer. In fact, there was hardly any daylight. Week after week, month after month, darkness gripped the world.

This wasn't because there was something wrong with the sun, but rather because of volcanism in distant Iceland.

A year without sun would spread terror now. It might well cause the collapse of modern civilization. Roman society, ruled as it was by superstition and with no idea that the eruption of an enormous volcano in a distant land was the source of the catastrophe, almost disintegrated.

Not just the Roman Empire, but the entire planet was plunged into a darkness that lasted for eighteen months. Temperatures plunged. The lack of light caused Vitamin D levels to drop in populations across the entire planet, and in 541 yet another plague erupted in the tottering remains of the Roman Empire.

The Plague of Justinian was the worst pandemic humanity had endured up to that time, and may be the worst in history, perhaps exceeding even the Black Death of the fourteenth century in terms of the number of people it killed. A hundred years before in the high plains of central Asia, a bacterium with the scientific name of *Yersinia pestis* had begun decimating the population. Bubonic Plague had arrived.

Ironically, the Western empire had been restored by the

current emperor, Justinian, primarily due to the success of his remarkable general Belisarius, who succeeded in destroying the Gothic kingdoms in North Africa and Italy. Justinian had also created a new set of laws known as the Code of Justinian, which remain to this day influential in the legal systems of some countries. Perhaps due to the influence of his wife, Theodora, he passed numerous reforms in support of the rights of women, including a stipulation that female prisoners would be guarded by women in order to prevent abuse. He also passed laws protecting prostitutes from exploitation, and women from being forced into prostitution. In addition, husbands were prohibited from taking on significant debts without their wives giving consent two times.

Documenting the plague, the historian Procopius described the characteristic buboes—swollen lymph nodes, as we now know—that appeared on infected individuals. Contagion spread so fast and was so quick-acting that people believed that the disease must be transmitted by sight. The Black Death would cut the population of Europe by as much as 60 percent. The Plague of Justinian did the same, and may done even worse, killing as many as 7 out of 10 Romans.

Procopius, a classical traditionalist, saw the plague as a mystery of nature. Another chronicler, John of Ephesus, who was a Christian and deeply involved in the continuing debate about the true nature of Jesus, saw it as a punishment levied by God on mankind for the sins of the people. In other words, one author approached it with a modern sensibility but little information, the other with the ancient idea that it had something to do with the anger of his god.

People poured into places of worship to beg forgiveness. They thought that the end of time had come, and when more volcanism took place in 451—452, it must have seemed certain to the now Christianized Roman Empire that God and Jesus had abandoned it. If the sun was blotted out today at the same time that a highly contagious and rapidly lethal plague was raging, billions of people would agree with John that God was angry with us. Others would agree with Procopius, with the difference that modern science would leave no doubt as to the origin of the catastrophe.

The Plague of Cyprian was a significant factor in the generalized abandonment of the old polytheism, but the Justinian Plague, which was far worse and accompanied by what must have been a terrifying darkness as well as dreadful cold and famine, shook but did not destroy Christianity.

There are probably two reasons for this. First, there was the Christian world's strong sense of community. Second, Christian belief had a highly developed concept of sin, which the old religions did not. So blame did not fall on God, but rather on sinful people, and the religion was only made stronger by the catastrophe.

The disease would abate, then return, then abate again, only to return yet again. Between 542 and 747, there were seven and possibly eight outbreaks in various parts of the empire. The last recurrence in the 740s was perhaps the worst of all. It started in the Umayyad Caliphate and moved north into Italy, then eastward to Constantinople. This time, the death rate was so enormous that the emperor had to force people to come in from the countryside to repopulate the city. The Eastern Roman Empire's population dropped from about 28 million to something like 8 million.

Roads fell into disuse. Aqueducts fell into disrepair or were pulled down by barbarians, money disappeared, and with it the Roman military and government.

By the eighth century, civilization in Western Europe had fallen into the long sleep of the religious dictatorship from which it would not awaken for a thousand years.

Did the strange, god-besotted man who had cried out the Beatitudes so long ago have anything to do with the disappearance of science and even thought itself into the prison of religious doctrine? Or was it some other force entirely, not only climate, but the human reaction to catastrophe that caused it?

Human beings quite naturally react with fear to disasters that they cannot control, and that is what destroys love and dignity and all the graces of human society and life.

Still, even given this fantastic succession of catastrophes, Christianity survived. For all his faults, Constantine had created the single most enduring social institution in the history of mankind. The sacrament established by Jesus was at its heart, but unlike other religions, it was also a way of life, and not just for clergy, but for every Christian. Through the plague and the darkness, the sickness and starvation, the Christian communities prevailed. In the face of invasions by outsiders with no idea at all of what civilization meant and no interest in preserving it, Christian monasteries held in reserve the writings of the past, the bits and pieces that were left from the old civilization, and the doctrinally acceptable documents from their own.

Jesus, who had been anointed as a living dead man by a woman, who had died and afterward been the beneficiary of some unknown power, disappeared into Christ, a distant god like all the others who had come before him, supposedly in control of nature and demanding worship in return for a beneficent life. The bizarre and challenging teacher of the Thomas and Mary gospels was buried along with the gospels themselves.

Mankind went on, struggling to survive chance encounters with nature as if they were punishments from an exalted and distant Christ. But the truth was and is that the mystery of Jesus, while it may in some way be a divine mystery, is certainly a human one. The ability that he demonstrated to understand the good and transcend death belongs to every one of us. Behind the walls of worship we have built around Christ is a man called Jesus, whose voice has been raised once again with the recovery of the gospels of Mary and Thomas, and whose mysterious burial garment bears an impression that suggests that something that surely must be impossible actually happened.

Even if he did somehow walk out of his tomb after his death, his actions before and after that event are not those of an all-seeing god, but rather of a man, a genius and a true master, but just as confused about the real nature of the world in which he lived, and just as erratic in his prophecies, as any other human being who was alive then might have been.

So his resurrection does not mark him as someone with more than normal knowledge of the world he lived in. His prophecies are too flawed to be the pronouncements of a divine being. His failure to realize things like the way words such as "render unto Caesar" would be misunderstood suggest that his brilliant mind also had very human limitations. Additionally, he did not know the future, or he wouldn't have prophesied as he did. 'Truly I tell you, this generation will certainly not pass away until all these things have happened." (Matt. 24:34) Just before saying that, he announced that "there will appear the sign of the Son of Man in heaven," and that he will gather in the elect. This caused a general expectation among his followers that the end of the world was shortly to happen. But it was not the infallible prediction of a deity, but rather the fervent belief of a religious ecstatic. It was, in other words, a human statement.

And yet, he *was* very extraordinary. Not only was he brilliant, he was also in possession of, or subject to, some absolutely incredible secret knowledge.

In this distant age, the Shroud challenges us not only to face the mystery of Jesus, but at the same time to face what may be an even greater one: if he could do that, then what are human beings?

15

THE LIGHT OF THE WORLD

As the greatest empire the world had ever known slipped into the past, the Thomas and Mary gospels lay buried in a clay pot in Egypt, and the Shroud hidden in a wall in a dying city on that empire's edge. Perhaps they were waiting for a moment that they could return and this time be understood. If so, that moment is now.

Not until our time, when the planet is changing again, with the same sort of cataclysmic weather, economic dislocation, restless migrations and pandemics that brought the empire down, have they re-emerged. Thomas and Mary bring forth the sterling message of how to find peace and power in oneself, and the Shroud challenges us to face the mystery of a man who walked twice among the living, and by doing so, face also the mystery of ourselves.

If we say that he could do what he did because he was God, then we have to ask another question: What is this God like, who could accomplish miracles and raise the dead, but who could not prophesy accurately?

The truth of the matter is that the age-old debate about whether Jesus was God or man has never been the correct way to approach the question. Jesus possessed the powers of a god but was subject to the limitations of a man. He wasn't god become man or god in man at all. He was a man in whom were unleashed hidden powers of mind and body.

I must confess that I have had a hard time with what has been discovered about the Shroud. I have had to reconcile myself to the idea that my humanity as I know it is apparently only a small part of what is there. To me, the fact that Jesus became more means that we all *contain* more.

I think that we are just at the beginning of what might well be one of the most important human journeys ever undertaken, which will involve our reaching beyond the limitations of materiality in ways that will reveal to us that we are not only part of the material world, but also of a much larger reality, the nature of which we have for all these long ages hidden from ourselves.

Flawed though Jesus was—confused, contradictory, and in many ways simply wrong—through his core teaching he laid down a path that is deeply freeing because it is morally pure. It can bring peace to anybody who finds a place for it in the secrecy of their own heart, and with that peace, under the right circumstances, I think that it can also open the door to mysterious powers within us, as it did to some extent for some of his students, who also became miracle workers.

His instruction that, if we understand his way, we will not "taste death" does not mean that the body won't die, but that its inevitable end will become part of what we accept always and in every moment, not something that we assume is somewhere far off in an indistinct future. I don't think that he rose from the dead so much as was able to project into the physical world what we all become after death.

"I am the light of the world." (John 8:12) It seems like the statement of somebody with an out-of-control god complex, and, as we have seen, Jesus was so deeply convinced that he had a special relationship with God that he could accomplish cures because of it, and after death even project a nonphysical aspect of himself into the physical world.

This all has to do with light, and suggests, along with other, related events that there is something more to this energy than we have as yet understood.

His relationship to light is fundamental to his story, and is the reason that the story survived at all. In fact, the entire journey toward the idea of God as a single, discrete presence is also a journey toward what must be a form of energy that is somehow conscious and appears in human eyes as living light.

In his stunning novel *Star Maker,* the great British science fiction writer Olaf Stapledon speculates that stars themselves may be imbued with an enormous, almost timeless consciousness, and that we may be perceivable to them, but only as a flicker in the immense time of their lives.

The belief that light is itself a holy being enters history with the Egyptian pharaoh Akhen-Aten in around 1350 B.C. Upon becoming pharaoh, he upended Egyptian religion by announcing that the sun was god and he was its missionary. Of course, there were undoubtedly solar deities before Akhen-Aten announced his theology, but his is the first solar religion of the historical period.

Possibly around the same time, although this is in question, an Iranian priest called Zoroaster encountered a shining figure he called Good Purpose, who taught him about Ahura Mazda, the Lord of Light. He spent the rest of his life attempting to convince people to follow the way of Asha, or order, that had been taught him by the entities of light. Early Zoroastrians did not use altars or texts, but rather turned toward a source of light when they worshiped.

Moses was also transformed by an incident involving light. "... the angel of the Lord appeared to him in flames of fire from within a bush." (Ex. 3:2) God then speaks to him from the fire, giving him instructions about leading his tribe out of Egypt, thus furthering the long journey of the Jews to the decision that the universe was created by a single god.

As we have seen, the transfiguration of Jesus before the apostles Peter, James and John involved light, and Paul was transformed from a persecutor of the followers of Jesus into a missionary for him when "suddenly a bright light from heaven flashed around me." (Acts 22:6)

Over the vast sweep of time from Akhen-Aten to Paul, then, incidents involving light essentially remake the religious character and culture of the Western world, and with it the structure of the civilization. They start with a pharaoh recognizing the sun as god and end when Jesus, in the form of light that speaks to Saul of Tarsus, completely overturns his mind, transforming him into the apostle Paul, who then spreads a version of the Jesus teaching into the gentile world. This new concept of God and morality eventually overturns the age old classical civilization, replacing it entirely.

So what is going on here? Is light itself conscious? If so, then did Stapledon—as has more than one fictional prophet—touch on something real in *Star Maker*?

It is not necessary to answer that question to conclude that it can be logically surmised that visions of entities composed of light have consistently inspired people to proclaim new religions. Further, in the cases I have described above, motive has also been consistent: to communicate the idea of a single god and, in the case of Paul, to add a complex moral teaching that was apparently communicated to him by unknown parties after the light temporarily blinded him.

All of the people who have come away with messages from the light have, in one way or another, been attempting to communicate with it. Akhen-Aten worshiped it. Zoroaster was wandering through the wilderness seeking enlightenment. Moses was begging for help. I think that Jesus, with his passionate assurance that he was connected to God, his dedication to his purpose and the great intelligence and compassion of his teaching, attracted the support of this energetic level of consciousness and it embraced his cause and helped him.

I think that it stands ready, as we move ever deeper into a future that may well come down to a struggle for the survival of the species, to intervene again, to support us on our journey toward a new and transcendent life. By transcendent, I mean a life in which we are all filled with compassion for one another and all that is, joined together on behalf of all of us and each of us and every living thing.

Jesus preached "love one another." So, did he know that his own church would become, in addition to one of the great forces for good in the world, also an engine of murder and oppression? He preached "be as little children," but that innocence did not continue for long among those who claimed to represent him on Earth.

"If you do not wake up, I will come like a thief. . ." The Roman world did not wake up, suffering its final death throes during the horrific volcanic winter of 536 and the Plague of Justinian that followed.

Given the fact that we are in the early stages of another era of profound disruption, it seems important to ask if the life and afterlife of Jesus suggests that there are powers dormant within us that might be awakened and used in some way, both for personal benefit and the benefit of all.

When the Council of Nicea declared Jesus a god, this very human question ceased to mean what it should have, and to this day doesn't resonate with its full meaning. A human being died on the cross. A few days later—which he *had* correctly predicted—a form walked out of his tomb and proceeded to spend more than a month interacting with a group of his disciples. This inspired them to embrace his teaching to the point of giving their lives to it and for it. As a result, they created a community based around his concepts of compassion and the idea that all human beings have value. This community has proved to be so strong that it continues to this day, and stands even now as a model of the type of human community that will be needed to endure the upheavals that are beginning to unfold all around us right now.

As much as we need to shake off the assumption that what happened to Jesus after his death is unknowable, we need to also get past the intellectual failure that dogs science, which is that phenomena that it cannot detect don't exist.

The history of science is a history of rejecting evidence until discoveries make it impossible to ignore. The history of Christianity is a history of asserting that the works and fate of Jesus are beyond human understanding.

Both approaches are flawed. There are no miracles that somehow defy nature. There are only natural phenomena that we understand and natural phenomena that we don't.

When there is proper testing of the Shroud, what we are almost certain to find is that Jesus turned into a version of himself made of light. He may have appeared human to those who saw him, but he was no longer an organic being. What happened was that a rare energetic event occurred that projected him back into the world for a time.

Perhaps if we could learn more about that secret band who seems to have been behind his passion and resurrection, and probably his whole life, that would help, but at the present time there appears to be no way to do that.

If we are willing to use the scientific tools we already have in a careful and properly designed analysis of the Shroud, we will be able to discover the truth of it, and thus also engage in disciplined speculation about the energy burst involved, and at least manage some intelligent speculation about how and why it caused a form that appeared to be Jesus to walk out of the tomb after his death.

I think that there was a consciousness with high intelligence behind the resurrection event and all the other incidents of light that I have discussed. There may have been a hidden organization as well, that was secretly in communion with this presence. I think that part of the message of the Shroud is that, by following the Jesus path, we all have the potential to enter the same state of light that he did.

To do this, we need to reconnect with Jesus as a teacher. We must no longer push away the potential of our own humanity by saying that he was a god, and thus that the states he displayed as a miracle worker and later as a man made of light, are impossible for us to attain. We have to ask ourselves, what do his teaching, his miracles and his resurrection tell us about our own powers?

This conscious energy—this light—is concerned about us or it would not intervene in our lives. Of course, it may be that it is part of us, but if that is true, then it is expressing a long term aim of which, in our normal lives, we are unaware. It has been making an effort to do three things: first, to channel our understanding in the direction of there being a single God; second to add depth and dimension to our concept of that deity, leading toward the idea that every human being has the right to and the responsibility for a direct relationship with it; third, to open up the possibility that we can, every one of us, follow the example of Jesus and in some way transcend death.

But how can we relate to a consciousness that does not have a nature that we can understand or even a form that we can detect? We can know that it *does* have an intense, ages-long interest in us, and from the way it has reacted in the past to our efforts to build relationship with it, we can be assured that it is aware of us and our efforts to commune.

Inwardly, the Jesus journey is toward self-empowerment, outwardly, toward the same transcendent relationship with the light that he had.

We have never in all our history had a concept of god that is not sentimentalized in some way like the vague idea of "God the Father," or personalized like the old gods of the Romans and the Egyptians. There is every reason now for that to change.

When at last you let go of beliefs and replace them with the central, unspoken question that lies at the heart of our whole relationship to reality, what you see of the truth is the immensity of suffering and love that is life now and history, too—the journey of humankind in the sweep of the ages. Belief or faith or none, it does not matter: Jesus is there.

The End

THE BEATITUDES

Beloved are the spiritual searchers, for they will be welcome in heaven.

Beloved are the sad, for they will be made cheerful.

Beloved are the gentle but strong, for the Earth is theirs.

Beloved are those who search for peace, for they shall find it.

Beloved are the compassionate, for they shall receive compassion.

Beloved are those who do not hate, for God shall be their companion.

Beloved are those who make peace, for they will be called children of God.

Beloved are the persecuted, for the dominion of heaven is open to them.

BIBLIOGRAPHY

Ancient and Classical Sources

Note: Most biblical quotations are from the New International Version, Grand Rapids, MI: Zondervan, 1973 and 1978; new editions, 1984 and 2011). Some are from the King James Version.

Apuleius. *The Florida* (The Place of Flowers). In *The Works of Apuleius*. Translated by Frank H. Cilley. London: Bell and Daldy, 1866.

Celsus, Aulus Cornelius. *On Medicine*. Translated by W. G. Spencer. Loeb Classical Library. Cambridge, MA: Harvard University Press, 1935, 1938.

Celsus. *On the True Doctrine: A Discourse Against the Christians*. Translated by R. Joseph Hoffmann. New York: Oxford University Press, 1987.

Cyprian of Carthage, Saint. *On the Mortality*. Translated by Robert Ernest Wallis. In *Fathers of the Third* Century, vol. 5 of *Ante-Nicene Fathers*, edited by Philip Schaff, Alexander Roberts, Sir James Donaldson, and Arthur Cleveland Coxe. Buffalo, NY: Christian Publishing Company, 1885.

Didache. Translated by M. B. Riddle. In *Early Church Fathers*, vol. 7 of *Ante-Nicene Fathers*, edited by Philip Schaff, Alexander Roberts, Sir James Donaldson, and Arthur Cleveland Coxe. Buffalo, NY: Christian Publishing Company, 1885.

Eusebius. *The History of the Church: From the Life of Christ to the Conversion of Constantine.* Translated by Arthur Cushman McGiffert. New York: The Christian Literature Co., 1890.

Eusebius. *Life of Constantine.* Edited and translated by Averil Cameron and Stuart G. Hall. Clarendon Ancient History Series. Oxford, UK: Clarendon Press, 1999.

Galen. *On the Natural Faculties.* Translated by A. J. Brock. Loeb Classical Library. Cambridge, MA: Harvard University Press, 1916.

Gospel of Mary of Magdala: Jesus and the First Woman Apostle. Translated by Karen King. Santa Rosa, CA: Polebridge Press, 2003.

Gregory of Nyssa, Saint. *Life of Gregory the Wonderworker.* In *Saint Gregory Thaumaturgus: Life and Works,* translated by Michael Slusser, vol. 98 of The Fathers of the Church. Washington, DC: The Catholic University of America Press, 2010.

Infancy Gospel of Thomas. In: Montague Rhodes James, translator. *The Apocryphal New Testament.* Oxford: Clarendon Press, 1924.

Jerome, Saint. *The Letters of Saint Jerome.* Translated by W. H. Fremantle, G. Lewis, and W. G. Martley. New York: Christian Literature Publishing Company, 1892. Reprint: London: Aeterna Press, 2016.

Josephus, Flavius. *Antiquities of the Jews.* Translated by William Whiston, 1737.

Justin Martyr. *Dialog with Trypho.* Translated by Marcus Dods and George Reith. In *The Apostolic Fathers with Justin Martyr and Irenaeus,* vol. 1 of *Ante-Nicene Fathers,* edited by Philip Schaff, Alexander Roberts, Sir James Donaldson, and Arthur Cleveland Coxe. Buffalo, NY: Christian Publishing Company, 1885.

Minucius Felix. *Octavius*. Translated by Robert Ernest Wallis. In *Fathers of the Third Century*, vol. 4 of *Ante-Nicene Fathers*, edited by Philip Schaff, Alexander Roberts, Sir James Donaldson, and Arthur Cleveland Coxe. Buffalo, NY: Christian Publishing Company, 1885. Online at newadvent.org.

Origen Adamantus. *Contra Celsum*. Translated by Frederick Crombie. In *Fathers of the Third Century*, vol. 4 of *Ante-Nicene Fathers*, edited by Philip Schaff, Alexander Roberts, Sir James Donaldson, and Arthur Cleveland Coxe. Buffalo, NY: Christian Publishing Company, 1885.

Philostratus. *The Life of Apollonius of Tyana*. Translated by Frederick Cornwallis Conybeare. New York: Macmillan, 1912. Reprint: CreateSpace Independent Publishing, 2011. Translated by Christopher P. Jones. Loeb Classical Library. Cambridge, MA: Harvard University Press, 2005.

Pliny the Elder. *Naturalis Historia (Natural History)*. Translated by H. Rackham, W. H. S. Jones, and D. E. Eichholz. Loeb Classical Library. Cambridge, MA: Harvard University Press, 1938. *Natural History: A Selection*. Translated by John F. Healy. New York: Penguin Classics, 1991.

Pliny the Younger. *Letters of the Younger Pliny*. Translated by Betty Radice. Loeb Classical Library. Cambridge, MA: Harvard University Press, 1969. Reprint: New York: Penguin Classics, 2003.

Protoevangelium of James. In: Montague Rhodes James, translator. *The Apocryphal New Testament*. Oxford: Clarendon Press, 1924.

Pseudo-Philo. *The Biblical Antiquities of Philo*. Translated by M. R. James. New York: Ktav Publishing House, 1971. Reprint: Wentworth Press, 2019.

Sayings Gospel of Thomas. Quoted material ranslated by the author (W. S.).

Suetonius. *Lives of the Twelve Caesars: An Unexpurgated*

English Edition. Translated by Joseph Gavorse. New York: Modern Library, 1931.

Tacitus. *The Life of Cnaeus Julius Agricola*. Translated by Alfred John Church and William Jackson Brodribb. London: Macmillan, 1868. Reprint: In *The Complete Works of Tacitus*. New York: Random House, 1988.

Modern Works

Antonacci, Mark. *Resurrection of the Shroud: New Scientific, Medical and Archeological Evidence*. New York: M. Evans, 2000.

———— *Test the Shroud: At the Atomic and Molecular Levels*. Nashville, TN: Forefront Books, 2016.

Aslan, Reza. *Zealot: The Life and Times of Jesus of Nazareth*. New York: Random House, 2013.

Bagnall, Roger S. *Egypt in Late Antiquity*. Princeton, NJ: Princeton University Press, 1993.

Dabrowski, Kazimierz. *Personality-Shaping Through Positive Disintegration*. Boston: Little, Brown, 1967. Otto, NC: Red Pill Press, 2015.

Frazer, James George. *The Golden Bough*. London: Macmillan, 1890. Abridged edition first published 1922. Reprint: New York: Penguin, 1996.

Gibbon, Edward. *History of the Decline and Fall of the Roman Empire*. Six volumes. New York: Penguin Random House, 2010. (Originally published 1776–1789.) Abridged edition: New York: Penguin Classics, 2000.

Gove, Harry E. *Relic, Icon or Hoax? Carbon Dating the Turin Shroud*. Philadelphia: Institute of Physics Publishing, 1996.

Hahn, Johannes, Stephen Emmel, and Ulrich Gotter, *From Temple to Church: Destruction and Renewal in Local Cultic Topography in Late Antiquity*. Boston: Brill, 2008.

Hockney, David, *Secret Knowledge: Rediscovering the Lost Techniques of the Old Masters*. Expanded edition. New York: Avery / Penguin Random House, 2006.

Hume, David, *An Enquiry Concerning Human Understanding.* 1748.

Jefferson, Thomas. *Life and Morals of Jesus of Nazareth Extracted Textually from the Gospels (The Jefferson Bible).* 1819. St. Louis, Chicago, and New York: N. D. Thompson, 1902.

Laurie, S. P., *The Thomas Code: Solving the Mystery of the Gospel of Thomas.* London: Hypostasis, 2018.

Rega, Frank M. *Padre Pio and America.* Chula Vista, CA: Aventine Press, 2004.

Smith, Morton, *Clement of Alexandria and a Secret Gospel of Mark.* Cambridge, MA; Harvard University Press, 1973, 2014.

Stapledon, Olaf, *Star Maker.* London: Methuen, 1937.

Tegmark, Max. *Our Mathematical Universe: My Quest for the Ultimate Nature of Reality.* New York: Alfred A. Knopf, 2014.

Theological Dictionary of the New Testament. Edited by Gerhard Kittel and Gerhard Friedrich. Ten volumes. Grand Rapids, MI: Wm. B. Eerdmans, 1977.

Watterson, Meggan. *Mary Magdalene Revealed: The First Apostle, Her Feminist Gospel, and the Christianity We Haven't Tried Yet.* Carlsbad, CA: Hay House, 2019.

Wilson, Ian. *The Shroud of Turin: The Burial Cloth of Jesus Christ?* New York: Doubleday, 1978. Revised and updated edition: *The Shroud.* London: Bantam Books, 2010.

Graves, Kersey. *The World's Sixteen Crucified Saviors: Or, Christianity Before Christ.* New York: The Freethought Press Association, 1875. Reprint: Compass Circle, 2020.

Wrede, William. *The Messianic Secret.* Translated from the German by J. C. G. Greig. London: James Clarke, 1971.

Yogananda, Paramahansa, *Autobiography of a Yogi.* Los Angeles: Self-Realization Fellowship, 1994.

INDEX

Z

Lightning Source UK Ltd.
Milton Keynes UK
UKHW020144271022
411147UK00001B/21/J